SUSAN ADAMS'

How-To-Cook

BOOK

SUSAN ADAMS'

How-To-Cook

BOOK

A. A. WYN, INC., NEW YORK

Printed in the United States of America
American Book–Stratford Press, Inc., New York

Dedicated to

H. L. M.

MY VERY PATIENT HUSBAND

Contents

SUSAN ADAMS'

How-To-Cook

BOOK

1. Introduction

Kitchen business requires a plan. As sure as you're born, those folks who seem to turn out a meal with a simple twist of the wrist . . . they had a plan!

This is a peaceful afternoon. Dinner is all planned; as a matter of fact, dinner got off to a good start this morning, when there was time to get the dessert into the refrigerator. Time now to check menus for the week end. Time now to check supplies and make out grocery lists. Time now to plan, so that tomorrow will go just as smoothly as today.

It takes planning to straighten out a kitchen so that it has good working space. It takes a plan to collect efficient cooking tools and equipment, in order to do a good job. It takes planning to learn *How-to-cook* each separate good dish for a meal. It takes planning to make a budget stretch. Every woman knows that these simple things make up the order and happiness of her home life. It takes planning to make days come out right for each and every member of the family.

Once you get this *methodical* approach to the business of cooking and housekeeping, then you begin to have time to polish up your *How-to-do's*. You soon discover that good food is invariably based on a collection of good patterns for cooking.

Speaking of good cooking patterns, take biscuits for instance. If you have a good biscuit pattern, then you can easily make delightful quick cinnamon rolls; you can make old-fashioned strawberry shortcake, so light, crisp, and tender it actually does melt in your mouth. You can make a savory meat pie or crisp meat turnovers. There is nothing to equal that basic pattern for laying the foundation.

This is where I come in! Do let me share my cooking patterns with you. In this book I am giving you basic patterns for breakfast, dinner, and that "little meal," which may be lunch, or supper, together with their recipes. Just as thousands of other homemakers have done and are doing, you will learn these basic How-To-Do recipes and depend on them.

Now—*this is a deal*—if you will conscientiously follow every detail and master each design in these patterns you will have the fundamentals of all good cooking at your finger tips.

With these fundamentals mastered, you can branch out into the most elaborate menus with no hesitation, *for elaborate menus are simply fundamentals with frills.*

Every woman knows that her basic dress is the most valuable gown in her wardrobe. Once you invest in this dress, variations are simple. This is just as true for basic food patterns. When you learn to poach an egg so perfectly that the golden yolk stands firmly in the center of the jellylike tender white portion (that's the trick to learn!), then it is no trouble at all to astonish and delight the family and friends with Eggs Benedict, the simple dish that acts so sophisticated.

Are you coming along?

COOKING EQUIPMENT
Helpful and Efficient

Whether you are an old hand at the business of home-making or a beginner in the kitchen, I am sure you will agree there is no substitute for good tools. Always purchase the best-quality equipment you can afford. This does not always mean the most expensive and certainly not the fanciest. Here are some helpful rules to follow in your selections:

POTS AND PANS

Be sure to choose pots and pans that use heat efficiently. By this I mean choose *pot and pans with straight sides,* with *heavy bottoms that will not warp* and tilt over heating unit, with *handles that are flame-proof,* with *handles that will not slip* (assurance against spilling). Purchase *sizes of pans* that will *cover a heating unit* and so use all of the heat.

Another thing, about *sizes of pans*—and this has to do with the amount the pan holds—remember that a small family needs large-sized equipment as well as small. The bride may use a two-egg frying pan, but there must also be a large frying pan, a whole-meal frying pan, in which to prepare a Swiss steak or a fricassee for two (or maybe for four). There must be a kettle large enough to stew a chicken as well as a small saucepan to cook a half pound of peas.

You do not have to start with a long list of kitchen equipment, but you need some tools which are exactly right.

A good rotary beater, ball-bearing and of fine construction. It will cost around $5.00, but will last indefinitely. This kind of rotary beater does a good job. Cheap light beaters do a cheap light job.

A set of fine steel knives, including medium, small, heavy, long, light, and large. A chef owns his own knives and permits nobody else to touch them. So should you.

A perforated turner shaped to lift eggs from water.

A long-handled perforated pancake turner.

A slotted spoon.

A very flexible wide spatulalike turner, which you'll find a lifesaver a dozen times each day.

A good strong wire whip (or "whisk") to beat egg whites for meringues, angel cakes, and mixtures of greater volume. Much more easily used when large quantities are beaten.

A small light wire beater to use for blending and mixing gravies, sauces, egg yolks, soups. I've used mine every meal for fifteen years. A must.

A wooden spoon with a long narrow bowl (not one with a round bowl). Wonderful for beating all batters, creaming all mixtures, stirring everything. You may have the deuce of a time finding these last three, but keep hunting—you'll love 'em.

A good strong wall can opener.

A good bone-handled two-tined fork.

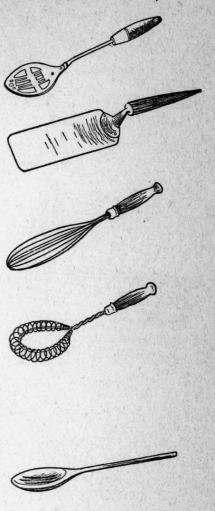

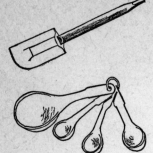

A long-handled rubber plate scraper.

A set of measuring spoons—¼, ⅓, ½, 1 teaspoon.

A set of measuring cups—¼, ⅓, ½, 1 cup.

A 2-cup sifter.

A large sifter.

A chopping board.

A coarse, medium, and fine grater set.

A set of Pyrex measuring cups— 1 cup, 1 pint, 1 quart.

BASIC MUSTS—SMALL EQUIPMENT FOR MEASURING, MIXING, AND GENERAL PREPARATION

1 pair scissors
2 pastry cloths
2 pastry brushes
2 sifters (1 large and 1 small)
2 pastry bags (large one and small one)
1 flat wire whisk
1 rotary beater
1 set Mary Ann measuring cups
1 set Pyrex measuring cups
2 spatulas—1 small and 1 large
2 French wire whisks—1 large and 1 small
2 broad short-handled turners
2 slotted wooden spoons
1 slotted egg spoon
1 slotted large spoon for folding
1 French pepper grinder
1 nutmeg grinder
2 biscuit cutters (1 large and 1 small)
3 sieves (small, medium, and large)
1 apple corer
1 two-tined fork
1 set of graters (3 pieces, fine, medium, and coarse)
1 colander

BASIC COOKING EQUIPMENT WHICH ENABLES A HOMEMAKER TO PREPARE ANY KIND OF A MEAL

*Equipment marked ** are "Musts" to start. Add remaining as soon as possible.*

** 1 large aluminum skillet with seal edge and tight lid, for braising, stews, casserole combinations

   1 large aluminum chicken fryer

** 1 Dutch oven, aluminum preferably

   1 set of iron or copper or aluminum skillets, small, medium, large

** 1 set aluminum saucepans, *heavy,* with lids

   1 three-gallon kettle, aluminum, with lid

   1 set round cake pans, 9-inch

** 1 set square cake pans, 8-inch

** 2 aluminum pie pans, 9-inch

** 2 cookie sheets (one is a must)

** 2 wire cake coolers

   1 jelly-roll pan

** 2 sets mixing bowls

   1 loaf-size Pyrex dish

** 2 shallow baking dishes, Pyrex, large and medium (one is a must)

** 3 casseroles, Pyrex (large, medium, and small)

   1 Pyrex double boiler

   1 set flame-ware Pyrex

** 1 four-cup coffee maker, glass

   1 eight-cup coffee maker, glass

   2 earthenware teapots

   1 large shallow roasting pan

MENU PLANNING

Menus for a Week Save Time, Effort, and Money

There are more good arguments for planning menus by the week than you might suppose at first glance. This is one of the sure ways to *eliminate monotony*. It really proves interesting and easy to think up seven interesting menus.

Planning menus by the week is *also thriftier*. Often you can take advantage of a larger cut of meat at a lower price by the pound, having the market man cut it into several types of servings. You may have chops one day from a cut of lamb or pork and store the roast to be cooked several days later.

Leftovers really become planned-overs when menus are planned ahead.

You can *take advantage of bargain buying in staples* when you know what you will need for the week.

Menu making for the week makes it possible to *check up* in a general way *on the nutrition of your meals*. You can see whether or not you are including sufficient raw and cooked vegetables and fruits in the family diet. You know whether there are enough milk dishes, such as cheese, custards, ice creams, served at home through the week to make up for any careless lack of milk drinking away from home.

Never for an instant think that once you have planned menus for a week you must stick to them religiously. Menus, like train schedules, are subject to change without notice. Maybe the planned-overs are so good that nothing is left over for the second dish. Possibly unexpected company calls for a change. You will often make changes because of better buys you find when you go to market.

Even with many changes, that planned week of menus will serve as a good take-off, a good pattern for the week to make cooking simpler and easier. It's like having money in the bank.

some menu-making tips

· plan menus when *you* are hungry
· plan menus at some quiet moment when you have time to look at a magazine or consult your cookbook for ideas
· why not plan some of your menus around family favorites; for instance, Dad's special cherry pie or the first strawberry shortcake; or maybe it's my rich vegetable soup—see page 93. These make the rest of the meal fall into line
· promise yourself to try something new each week and plan it into a menu
· get acquainted with international neighbors and use some of their food ideas to make your menus more interesting
· plant herbs in a window box, or in your garden, and adventure with seasonings that are your own; new dishes are developed this way
· don't wait to invite a friend for dinner or lunch—do it now. Then you will be forced to polish up a menu

marketing for the menu

· Make daily market list and watch the grocery ads

- do, please, market at "slack" hours, usually mid-morning or mid-afternoon, when you can take time to shop the featured items; also, when you can take time to discuss meat cuts, get information about seafood and similar foods
- form the habit of reading the labels on packages of food. The information given there has been carefully compiled for you by experts; take advantage of that service
- compare prices of competitive products; check quality, size, and weight

GET READY
TO SERVE A GOOD MEAL

There is nothing that adds so much to the pleasure of a good meal as the manner in which it is served. I am not referring to the service of a formal meal (how many people serve a formal meal today?) But I do mean those small but specific attentions to detail which put the come-hither into the foods you serve, from breakfast straight on through the day.

Have you ever watched the waitress at your restaurant clearing her table for the day? She lays aside all the silver that needs polishing. She refills and cleans all salt and pepper holders; *sifts* new sugar into sugar bowls and cleans sirup pitchers and refills them. Then she uses a damp cloth to wipe clean the tops of catsup, mustard, and sauce bottles.

Doing these chores each day in your own home requires but a few minutes and saves hours of accumulated time, but even more important, you are always *ready* to set a beautifully appointed table.

Whatever linen or table mats are used, be very sure they are spotlessly clean and selected to make a flattering background for your menu. Even one gay flower floating in a glass bowl of water makes the table seem festive. Polished fruits or vegetables are artistic for table decorations and may be eaten tomorrow.

It is important to place silver straight and orderly at each side of plates. It is so easy to give a final polish to glasses so they'll gleam. It takes two minutes by the clock to run scalding hot water over plates or serving dishes before carrying them to the table. Good chefs always give special attention to having your plate hot. Isn't it important at *your* table too?

GET READY TO COOK

If I thought you would read it, do you know what I'd like to do? I would like to write a whole cookbook on

GET · READY · TO · COOK!

I was never more certain of anything than this: if you get all the preliminaries lined up first, before beginning to cook, success is certain in the kitchen. This is just as true for cooking some one simple thing (for instance, poaching an egg) as it is for preparing a whole meal. After all, what is a perfect meal but a collection of dishes each prepared perfectly? GET READY is the answer to many and many a cooking problem. Here are my most cherished suggestions:

Examples of How-to-get-ready To Cook

1. Plan menu and write it on paper.
2. Visualize the food on the table and on plates.
3. Start roast or vegetable or dessert which requires longest cooking time.
4. If preparing to make a pie, cake, or anything which requires several ingredients, get ready by reading the recipe through; then measure and assemble all ingredients on a tray. Make it a habit to close spice jars, boxes, etc., then remove each from tray as used. This serves as a double check for what you've used. When your tray is empty, there is no question in your mind about whether or not you did add that salt!
5. When making cakes always prepare pans *first*. Then batter or egg whites do not have to stand and lose quality.
6. When poaching eggs—*get ready* by heating water, then placing soft paper toweling, with lifter and heated plate, near by.
7. How-to-get-ready to serve soft cooked eggs . . . Heat serving cups for eggs. Place knife, spoon, and a piece of soft paper near by.
8. How-to-get-ready to serve gravy . . . Heat gravy bowl and ladle very hot. Pour half of the bubbling hot gravy into bowl and serve *now*. Reheat remainder of gravy to serve for second helpings. Add a little more milk if it has thickened from standing. Nobody likes cold, thick gravy.
9. How-to-get-ready to serve broiled steak, baked po-

tato, and salad . . . Place potatoes in hot oven to bake from 45 minutes to 1 hour. Prepare salad and dressing, but mix at table. Keep chilled. Broil steaks, timing to be done when family sits down to table. Keep plates hot on oven, or run scalding hot water over them at last minute.

10. Check required foods in refrigerator and remove as many as practical at one time. This way your refrigerator is not opened too often.

WHAT DO YOU EAT?

Check yourself today and see if you've had your daily requirements. Of course each member of your family needs to know these musts, so why not put the list on your bulletin board each morning? This will be a guide for you as you plan menus.

Milk

Each adult needs one pint of milk each day. You may drink it or eat it in sauces, soups, cheese, or ice cream. Remember that 1/3 pound of cheese equals 1 quart of fluid milk in food value. Each child must have 1 quart of milk every day. Three in your family? Then you need at least 2 quarts of milk today and every day.

Lean Meat, Poultry, Fish

One serving each day of one of these. Study page 111, on meat cookery, and remember that the less tender and less expensive cuts of meat have the same nourishment expensive meats provide.

Vegetables

Two servings each day. This must include one leafy, green, or yellow vegetable besides potatoes. Raw vegetables in salads and carrots, celery, fennel, cucumbers, or radishes should be on your menus daily.

Fruits

Two servings at least and always include citrus fruits (oranges, grapefruit, lemons, or limes) or tomatoes each day.

Bread and Cereal

Two servings each day of whole-grain cereal or bread. This may be whole-wheat bread or rye or enriched bread. It may be oatmeal, brown rice, or cracked-wheat cereal.

Eggs

About 1 egg each day, say the experts. It may be in custards, sauces, or desserts. 3 or 4 eggs per week are minimum.

Fats

Two tablespoons of butter each day. Or margarine to which Vitamin A is added. Bacon is fat, you know, and not included in meat.

Sweets

Small amount always. You'll get sugar in preserves, desserts, candy, and sirup, so count them all.

2. Breakfast

WHY BREAKFAST?

What is the breakfast score in your family? Are yours the hearty breakfasters? Do you have an eat-and-run laggard, or a run-without-eating commuter? We've got to do something about that. Calorie counters are a problem, too.

There is no getting around it, breakfast is a *must*. The very word *breakfast* means to break a fast. Some six to eight, possibly ten to twelve hours have gone by since food has been eaten. And now at the breakfast hour it is time to fire the engine for the new half day of work that lies ahead.

May I suggest that you turn back to pages 23, 24, "Get Ready to Serve a Good Meal," and refresh your memory on the little wrinkles of service that can make a table more attractive? This is most important at breakfast time.

May I also call your attention to the good old bulletin board? It can be a sure 'nuff help in trouble. For instance, has it ever occurred to you to post the breakfast menu on a bulletin board (for yourself, of course, if anyone should inquire)—but notice how appetites can brighten when favorites are coming up. You might also try some "come-on" hints on the bulletin board—maybe a note to yourself to remember buckwheat flour for breakfast griddle cakes (with maple sirup!)

Best of all, first, last, and always SERVE A GOOD BREAKFAST. There is a time for good routine breakfasts (about four mornings out of every seven mornings every week!) But there is also time and place for surprise breakfasts; gay breakfasts; economy breakfasts. Try an "other-nations breakfast" once in a while.

Hot-weather breakfasts are sometimes mighty important. You could make a reputation for yourself with specialty breakfasts for Saturday or Sunday mornings when guests may drop in. In other words—get away from monotony at breakfast time. At the very end of this breakfast section there are a few typical menus to help solve some breakfast problems.

And again, first, last, and always, serve a good breakfast. The coffee should be perfect. Note special service hints for morning fruits, page 30. All breakfast dishes can be simple but well prepared. Even a breakfast plate can find a use for a sprig of watercress or mint, a slice of lemon, a crest of jelly, to enliven a dull morning.

BREAKFAST HOW-TO-DO'S

The recipes in this breakfast section are all basic recipes. By this I mean that the method of cooking outlined in each is basic to the preparation of that food. If you will take the time to master each one completely and perfectly, it will become a stepping stone to better and finer cooking. For once you learn these basic *How-to-do's* you can go from there to all kinds of combinations. You can do so much with these basic dishes!

Coffee

· we might start by saying that to learn to make good coffee is to acquire a very valuable social accomplishment. It is certainly one way to keep the man of the house in good humor. It wins laurels for you among all your friends. Learning to make a good cup of coffee is also basic to making many a good mocha dessert or sauce or frosting. Do take the time and trouble to learn HOW-TO-DO a fragrant brew.

Breakfast Fruits

· the preparation of breakfast fruits is obviously less elaborate than the preparation of those same fruits for dinner-table service. But to learn about combining juices and fruits in simple but attractive manner for the breakfast table will lead to better service and wider use of fruits at other hours of the day.

There are basic methods for cooking certain fruits, basic to their use in other combination dishes. Dried fruits, for instance—do you know how to cook these? There is a correct way that will secure best results, important in a fruit compote, important in making ice cream or a mousse.

Cereals

· the basic recipes for the cooking of cereals apply to the preparation of all starchy grain foods. And don't forget that well-cooked cereals are the basis for other favorite breakfast foods, such as fried cornmeal mush. Many dinner dishes are based on cereal cooking.

Breakfast Eggs

· egg cookery is based on certain definite rules that make for success. You do not learn these all at once. You master them day by day. So begin with breakfast eggs.

Breakfast Meats

learn to broil one strip of bacon and you have learned How-to-broil meat. Always keep your thinking straight about this business of how-to-broil. Broiling means Dry, Direct Heat. So keep that fat drained off as the bacon broils. You will later follow the same simple steps when you tackle a trout, a porterhouse, or a squab chicken.

Breakfast Breads

· breakfast breads have a luxurious sound. The very words suggest thoughtfulness and concern for your family. The basic patterns for their preparation are basic also to many main-dish and dessert favorites. It pays to take time to learn about doughs and batters. They are useful in all kinds of cooking.

GET READY
TO COOK AND SERVE BREAKFAST

Here it is again—Get Ready! There is nothing like having a breakfast plan, all set and ready to go, before you even begin to cook and serve a breakfast.

How-to-get-ready

Learn to use your oven to keep food hot. Turn heat low (about 200 degrees) and leave oven door partly open.

- toast should never be stacked (it will become moist and soggy). Place on wire cake cooler and keep hot in oven
- place broiled bacon on paper toweling. Keep hot in oven
- cups, saucers, plates can be warming on top or near top of oven

Get coffee ready—start it cooking just before you make the toast.

Make toast and keep it hot.

Broil bacon and keep it hot.

Scald cups and plates and keep hot.

Prepare eggs last step.

If you are new at meal preparation follow this order, step by step. Pretty soon the procedures will become automatic, and you will soon learn to keep these steps all going at the same time.

BREAKFAST PATTERNS

See what can be done with that standard pattern for an American breakfast that puts everyone in the mood for a good day.

Here is the basic pattern:

Fruit
Eggs and/or Cereals
Bacon, Ham, or Sausage (optional)
Coffee, Milk, or Tea
(But especially coffee)

And here are three designs based on this pattern (there are additional designs beginning on page 63).

DESIGN A

Orange or Grapefruit Juice
Oatmeal with Cream
All Bran Muffins with Butter
Coffee

DESIGN B

Stewed Fruit
(Fresh, Canned, Dried)
Package Cereal with Whole
Milk
Whole Wheat Toast, Buttered
Eggs and Bacon
(poached, scrambled, or soft-
cooked)
Coffee

DESIGN C

Fruit or Melon in season
French Toast or Waffles
or
Griddle Cakes
Broiled Ham or Sausage
Pecan, Raisin, or Date Muffins
Coffee

The perfection of breakfast depends on *how-you-do* each separate dish. Is your coffee lively, clear, and fragrant? Is the cereal good-textured? Are the eggs perfectly done? Learn how-to-do each breakfast serving. Don't stop until you have mastered each. Ask yourself—am I ready to prepare any breakfast for a panel of experts? If the answer is no—back to the kitchen.

HOW-TO-MAKE COFFEE

General Directions

Is there, anywhere, an American who does not harp on the subject of *good coffee?* And what is good coffee according to American standards? It is a fresh, fragrant brew, clear amber-colored and rich with flavor—emphasis on rich. There are general rules that apply to coffee making.

1. Coffee must always be tightly covered.
2. Drip grind must be used for glass coffee makers.
3. Buy correct grind for whatever utensil you have.
4. Always use fresh cold water, *never* water from tank or tea kettle (that is dead, stale water).
5. Coffee must never boil.
6. Never reheat coffee. When it is cold it is old, so throw it out.
7. Serve coffee hot.
8. If you can spare space, keep tightly covered can of coffee in refrigerator.

And with all of this you can still ruin coffee if you do not keep your coffee maker, or percolator, or whatever you are using, spotlessly clean. Wash it with soap and water, rinse well, air it, sun it—keep it clean!

How-to-do Coffee in a Vacuum Coffee Maker

1. Every vacuum coffee maker requires a minimum of 3 cups of fresh cold water. Use cold water from the faucet, not water from the hot-water tap or the tea-kettle.
2. Place water in bottom container.
3. Adjust top container and rod, or weight.
4. Using coffee measure, or tablespoon, measure 2 full tablespoons of drip grind coffee to each cup of water; place in top container.

5. Wipe bottom container dry and place over heat.

6. When water is forced to top and no more travels up the tube, remove coffee maker from heat. Coffee in top will be forced immediately into bottom container.

7. Serve—either black, or with real cream.

The water never boils in a vacuum coffee maker, even though it may have that appearance. The coffee maker is adjusted to keep the temperature never above 204 degrees and you know that water boils at 212 degrees.

Follow these coffee-making steps DAILY—CONSISTENTLY —UNFAILINGLY. Measure both water and coffee ACCU- RATELY. You will have perfect coffee 365 days a year.

How-to-do Percolated Coffee

1. Always use correct-size percolator for number served. Measure fresh cold water into percolator (never from hot-water tank).

2. Measure percolator-grind coffee into basket, allowing 2 tablespoons* to each cup of water.

3. Use medium heat until coffee begins to percolate, then lower flame and continue percolating from 8 to 10 minutes. Coffee will be light brown, or a rich amber shade. Serve immediately in heated cups, with good rich cream.

How-to-do Boiled Coffee

This method is misnamed—as the coffee does not boil.

---

* If you increase or decrease this amount to meet your personal taste, remember that you are setting up your own standard of measure and be sure to abide by it. Measure *your* required amount accurately.

1. Measure the coffee and measure the water into an old-fashioned coffeepot.
2. As soon as bubbles begin to break on the edge, stuff the spout with waxed paper, turn off the heat, and let coffee stand until it settles.
3. Pour carefully into heated cups.

HOW-TO-DO BREAKFAST FRUITS

Get into the habit of making breakfast fruit a real eye opener. There are the good standard fruits such as chilled orange juice, grapefruit in halves or juiced, and many others which you likely serve regularly. But there are some fruit servings that give the appetite a pleasant jolt of surprise. Here are a few of my favorites:

Mix-mates

- did you ever mix grapefruit juice with apricot nectar and serve it icy cold from a tall thin glass?
- did you ever slice ripe figs paper thin and serve them on a magnolia leaf or a big grape leaf—or on sprigs of watercress?
- did you ever whirl pineapple juice into a foaming froth, then just fill a glass pitcher for the family to help themselves—a few sprigs of mint will add to the come-on
- did you ever mix simmered dried apricots and prunes in a pretty glass bowl—maybe a bowl on a stem . . . shavings of preserved ginger or a couple of maraschino cherries, thinly sliced, add color and flavor interest
- did you ever slice oranges very thin and arrange them in a circle around a glass plate to eat with a fork?

• do you ever make an eggnog of orange juice—this calls for orange juice plus a raw egg, a teaspoon of honey, and a shot of lime juice (or lemon juice). No blender to do the mixing? Then take a Mason jar with a rubber and a lid and shake it hard

HOW-TO-DO NOTCHED MELON

Did you ever serve a notched melon? Just for variation try it for breakfast. Mighty easy. Very pretty.

> 1 cantaloupe
> 2 sections lemon or lime

1. Draw a line around the center of melon.
2. Using a sharp paring knife, cut a continuous line of "V's" around the melon, letting each side of each V extend half above and half below the center marking line.
3. Be sure to cut all the way through the rind.
4. Pull apart, remove seeds, and chill.
5. Serve with a section of lemon or lime.

One melon serves 2 to 4, depending upon size.

HOW-TO-DO PINEAPPLE FOR BREAKFAST

Pineapple is economical, delightful to eat, and so easy to prepare.

> 1 well-ripened pineapple
> ¼ to ½ cup sugar (to taste)

1. Select fresh, ripe pineapple. It is ripe when inside leaves or spines pull out easily.

2. On a chopping board, place pineapple on its side, stem end toward you.

3. Using a long, sharp knife, cut the bottom slice off.

4. Then cut into slices about one half inch thick. When fruit is sliced, use a sharp paring knife and peel around each slice, cutting out the eyes as you peel. Cut each circle in halves or fourths and remove the core.

5. Be sure to hold fruit over a bowl to save all the juice.

6. Add granulated sugar to taste, cover bowl, and set aside for an hour or more—NOT in the refrigerator.

7. When sugar has dissolved and been taken up by the pineapple, it may be chilled. However, the gourmet enjoys fruit at its normal temperature, for the flavor is much richer and more luscious.

One pineapple serves 4 to 8, depending upon size.

Serve in glass bowls for dessert, or for first course next time you have Sunday brunch. For breakfast service, pineapple may be prepared the night before.

If you want to use whole slices of pineapple, just cut out the center core after each slice is peeled.

HOW-TO-DO POACHED FRESH FRUIT

This is a recipe I learned to do on the third voyage of the *Normandie*. In their pretentious galleys this fruit was poached in huge covered boilers. Not any of the color, fragrance, or shape of the fruit was disturbed in this poaching process. Their recipe was for 1500 guests, but I reduced it to a serving for 4. Do try it once. Then I know you'll double the recipe next time.

4 peaches	8 plums
4 nectarines	2 dozen Bing cherries
4 apricots	4 cups water

1. Heat water in deep kettle and add 1 cup sugar, stirring until dissolved.
2. When liquid is boiling drop in the washed, but not peeled, peaches, nectarines, and apricots.
3. Let come to boil again, quickly. Cover.
4. Let fruit simmer for 12 minutes.
5. Using large slotted spoon, dip out apricots at the end of 6 minutes.
6. Place apricots in large deep bowl.
7. At the end of 8 to 10 minutes dip out nectarines and place in bowl with apricots.
8. At the end of 12 minutes, dip out peaches and add to bowl.
9. Now drop plums and cherries into kettle of boiling liquid.
10. These last fruits require only about 4 minutes. Don't cook long enough for skins to burst.
11. Dip them into bowl with other fruits.
12. To the juice add one cup more of sugar and stir till dissolved. Add a few drops of red fruit coloring to give the juice a rich deep-pink coloring.
13. Boil rapidly 5 minutes.
14. Pour over fruits in big bowl and add 2 teaspoons of lemon juice. Set aside to cool.
15. When cold, serve in glass dessert bowls about the size of soup plates. Give each person a peach, a nectarine,

an apricot, and two plums, together with several cherries and a generous amount of juice. Eat with dessert spoons. Delicious, and beautiful besides. Watch your markets for really ripe fruit. It's much more flavorful.

Serves 4 persons generously.

How-to-do a Grapefruit

1. Using a long, sharp knife start at the end and peel round and round. Use a kind of sawing cutting motion and peel deeply. Be sure every bit of that white portion comes off.
2. Now with a thin sharp knife cut down each side of the membrane which holds sections in place.
3. Carefully slip sections loose from fruit and ease them out. After the first section or two it's very fast and you'll have big whole sections of beautiful grapefruit for salads. Be sure to hold grapefruit over a bowl as you work so that juice is not lost. The juice is good too!

HOW-TO-DO BREADS

BISCUITS

You will need:

2 cups sifted flour	½ teaspoon salt
3 teaspoons baking powder	6 tablespoons shortening
⅔ to ¾ cup milk	

1. Sift dry ingredients together into deep bowl—flour, baking powder, and salt.

2. Measure and add 6 *level* tablespoons shortening and using pastry blender chop it into the dry ingredients until you have a mixture like very coarse meal.

3. Using a fork, stir almost all the milk into the dry ingredients until the dough follows a fork around the bowl without sticking to the sides of the bowl. Add the rest of the milk, if necessary, to make a very soft but not sticky dough.

4. Rub flour generously into pastry cloth and turn ball of dough onto this.

5. Fold dough over to center of ball and press lightly in kneading motion. Don't overdo this. Half a dozen light kneads are enough. Do not work any more flour into dough as you go. Extra flour kneaded into dough makes biscuits dry and tough.

6. Pat gently with your hand or roll lightly with rolling pin to about ½ inch in thickness.

7. Cut with floured cutter and place on ungreased baking sheet, about ½ inch apart, if you like them crisp, or touching if you like them soft. Bake 12 to 15 minutes on middle rack in your oven, which has been heated to 450 degrees. Serve piping hot. The Southern homemaker brings the tray of biscuits right out of the oven and passes them, always reminding you to "take two and butter 'em."

Serves 6 to 8.

Now, when you've mastered this basic biscuit recipe, you are ready for dumplings, meat pies, cobblers, strawberry shortcake, or any quick dough mixture.

The basic rules apply exactly the same: light handling; avoid adding additional flour; quick cooking.

Breakfast Biscuits

As you prepare dinner, stir up a panful of biscuits to store in your refrigerator until morning. Rub waxed paper generously with butter and fit it over the biscuits before storing away. At breakfast time, just slip the pan, paper and all, into the hot oven. The butter melts into the biscuit tops and they are crisp and delightful. Remove paper after butter has melted.

Muffins

MUFFINS are a batter-type hot bread.
The dry ingredients are sifted together.
The eggs and liquids are beaten together.
Then the two are quickly combined with the least possible stirring or mixing.

BLUEBERRY MUFFINS

These are my favorite, two-bowl muffins, made with twenty strokes. They may be varied by adding dates and other fruit instead of the blueberries. Or, add dates and pecans and brown sugar to the bottom of a custard cup, before pouring in the batter.

2 cups sifted flour	2 eggs
4 teaspoons baking powder	4 tablespoons melted butter
½ teaspoon salt	1 cup milk
4 tablespoons sugar	⅔ cup blueberries

1. BOWL I
Sift the flour, baking powder, salt, and sugar into one mixing bowl.

2. BOWL II
   Beat eggs until foamy; add melted butter, milk, and blueberries. Mix.
3. Quickly stir contents of Bowl II into Bowl I, using the fewest possible strokes. OVERMIXING is the pitfall of making muffins. Try to mix them with twenty strokes. Just don't see the lumps. They'll bake out and if you try to beat them out you'll surely have tunnels and leathery muffins.
4. Pour into oiled muffin pans, being careful to fill only 2/3 full.
5. Bake in 425-degree oven for from 20 to 25 minutes. Take out of the muffin pans just as soon as they are done and serve hot. *Makes 1 dozen medium-sized.* Omit blueberries for basic plain muffins.
   Serves 6 to 8.

HOW-TO-DO LIGHT, FEATHERY PANCAKES

This is my grandmother's recipe and although I've tried many others I always come back to this one.

1. BOWL I
   Sift 1½ cups flour with
     1½ teaspoons baking powder
     ½ teaspoon soda
     ½ teaspoon salt
     2 teaspoons sugar
     Dash nutmeg

2. BOWL II
   Using rotary beater, beat 2 egg yolks until pale lemon-colored
   Add 1⅔ cups fresh buttermilk
   [Grandmother used sour cream]
   Add 4 tablespoons melted butter

3. Using least number of strokes possible, stir ingredients of Bowl II into Bowl I.

4. Next, fold the 2 stiffly beaten egg whites through the batter. Be stingy with the mixing motions. Overmixing makes pancakes tough, instead of light.

*　　*　　*

To Bake on Hot Griddle:

5. First test griddle by sprinkling a few drops of cold water onto hot griddle. If drops dance around on surface, it's right.

6. Immediately pour batter from tip of spoon or from pitcher to form perfectly round, even cakes. Most griddles require no grease. A very light coating of grease, if any, is used.

7. As soon as cakes are covered on top with unbroken bubbles, turn and brown on other side. If you wait till the bubbles break the cakes will be dry.

8. NOTE: Turn cakes only once.
   Don't try to bake more than three at a time.
   Don't get batter too thick or cakes will be thick and heavy.
   Always serve from heated plate.
   Always have butter softened or melted.
   Don't keep in stacks. Bake only as served.

Serves 4 to 6.

HOW-TO-DO CRISP, BUTTERY WAFFLES

You will need:

2 cups sifted flour	2 tablespoons sugar
4 teaspoons baking powder	2 eggs
½ teaspoon salt	1¾ cups milk
8 tablespoons melted butter	

1. Sift flour, baking powder, salt, and sugar into one large mixing bowl.
2. Separate eggs, placing yolks in one bowl, whites in another.
3. Beat yolks with rotary beater until thick and lemon-colored. Add milk and butter.
4. Next, lightly fold the 2 stiffly beaten egg whites through the batter. Do not overmix.
5. Bake in hot waffle iron. Pour batter into center of iron and do not fill iron too full. As long as steam comes from iron, don't open.
6. Serve waffles on heated plate. Don't stack waffles. Let waffle iron stand open to cool.

These are crisp, delicious waffles and worth the cost. If you want to cut down, use half butter and half shortening.

Serves 4 to 6.

To Vary: Sprinkle pecans over batter in iron and bake as usual. Or drained blueberries may be added the same way. Crumbled broiled bacon gives a delicious waffle for creamed chicken. Mighty good for Sunday-night suppers.

HOW-TO-DO POPOVERS

It is really easy to make light crusty popovers which really pop. Of course, they're best freshly made, but they are also mighty good toasted and filled with creamed servings.

You will need:

2 eggs	2 teaspoons melted butter
1 cup milk	1/4 teaspoon salt
	1 cup flour

1. In a deep bowl, using a rotary beater, beat eggs until light and foamy.
2. Add milk, salt, and melted butter and beat together.
3. Now dump in the flour and beat hard until perfectly smooth, light, and bubbly.
4. Heat iron muffin pans, well greased, to sizzling hot. Glass custard cups may be used, also.
5. Fill 2/3 full of batter.
6. Bake in hot oven, 450 degrees, about 30 minutes, when they will have popped and will be high and brown.
7. Turn heat down to 350 degrees and bake for from 10 to 15 minutes more.
8. *Using sharp paring knife, cut a small slit in each one to let steam out.* This is important. It prevents sogginess.
9. Serve at once, or just place a pat of butter inside each popover and set them on baking sheet in hot oven for a few minutes.

Makes about 8 popovers.

HOW-TO-DO FRENCH TOAST

For breakfast or brunch, this is a very special kind of French toast. It is very easy to do and yet it seems new to all my guests. Each time I serve it I have to write out the recipe for my friends. Here it is for everyone.

You will need:

2 eggs
1 cup milk
Dash of salt
1 tablespoon brown sugar

1 loaf *unsliced* bread
   (2 or 3 days old)
Fat for deep-fat frying
Confectioners' sugar

1. Beat eggs slightly with a fork. Add milk.
2. Add salt and brown sugar and stir together.
3. Cut bread into slices about 2 inches thick. Remove crusts. Now cut each slice to make two long, thick blocks.
4. Dip each block, one at a time, into the egg-and-milk mixture, turning to coat all sides well. Drain, or blot against another block.
5. Fry in deep hot fat, turning once, until golden brown. Do not fry too long. Drain on soft paper.
6. Dust lightly with confectioners' sugar. Serve on folded napkin. Marvelous with fresh strawberry preserves. Not bad with shaved maple sugar, or honey, and sweet butter.

Serves 4 to 6.

Don't—try to use regular sliced bread
    soak bread in milk and egg mixture
    fry too brown
    be afraid of deep-fat frying, for it is easy. I just use my small copper skillet, which is rather deep, and put shortening in it to fill about 2/3 full. This provides plenty of surface. The fat can be strained after using, to be used again.

How-to-do Toasted English Muffins

1. First, pull the muffins apart. Don't cut, as that makes them packed and soggy.
2. Place them cut side down on broiler rack and heat for only a few minutes. They will not brown.

3. Remove, turn, and butter the cut side generously.

4. Run under broiler long enough to toast to a crusty golden brown with butter bubbling around the edges.

5. Serve immediately, with marmalade or strawberry jam.

HOW-TO-DO EGGS

FRIED EGGS

Not many folks realize it is an art to fry an egg properly. That is, to fry an egg so that it has regular form, is moist, not dry, is tender and delicate of texture. Learn how-to-do one fried egg, then whether you fry one egg at a time or one dozen, the results will always be the same—successful!

You will need:

> 1 egg
> 1 teaspoon butter
> Salt and pepper to taste

1. Use a small skillet, approximately 6 inches. In it melt 1 teaspoon butter, over low heat. Butter should be hot enough to prevent fat soaking into egg, but not hot enough to scorch, or to crust edge of egg white.

2. Drop egg into skillet.

3. Cover with a good tight lid. Continue cooking over low heat until egg white is jellylike in consistency, the yolk is set, and both are tender. Dust with salt and pepper; remove to warmed plate. (Egg may be turned once if you prefer.)

SCRAMBLED EGGS IN A SKILLET

4 eggs
4 tablespoons top milk or cream
1 tablespoon butter

1. Beat eggs with a rotary beater till light and foamy. Add milk or cream and beat again.
2. In heavy skillet, heat the butter, but watch closely, so that it does not brown. Turn eggs into skillet and cook slowly.
3. Tilt the skillet and then turn the egg, which has coated the bottom, letting the liquid run back and recoat the skillet.
4. Keep turning the egg from the bottom and piling it to one side of the skillet. Hold this side of skillet away from heat.
5. Soon the mixture may be rolled into an omelet-shaped roll and turned out onto a warmed plate. Do not overcook, for eggs should be moist, tender, and light.

Serves 2 to 3.

MY DOUBLE-BOILER SCRAMBLED EGGS

Somehow I especially like to do scrambled eggs "my way" —maybe you'll discover why.

You will need:

6 eggs   4 tablespoons butter
6 tablespoons cream   Salt and pepper to taste

1. In a deep bowl, using a rotary beater, beat eggs until very light and foamy.
2. Add cream, or top milk, and beat again lightly.

3. Heat butter in large skillet (never permit butter to brown).

4. Add eggs and let them heat to form a coating over the surface of the skillet. Add salt and pepper to taste.

5. Using a broad spatula, or a pancake turner, gently lift the coating over to one side of skillet and let the uncooked egg flow back.

6. Continue this until you have a mound of softly cooked egg mixture piled to one side of the skillet.

7. Keep the pile side off the heat and tilt the skillet to let all the uncooked portion flow to the heat side of skillet.

8. Shake skillet toward you to form a roll almost like an omelet. This will be very soft and light.

9. Now turn the moist, soft scrambled eggs into a well-buttered double boiler over warm (not hot) water. Cover and keep until time to serve. They will stay moist longer than you'd believe.

Serves 3 to 4.

Poached Eggs

As the water is heating in a skillet . . .

GET READY. Place soft paper napkin, slotted pancake turner, heated plate, and crisp toast close beside the skillet. Break eggs into a shallow bowl or plate. Turn heat to low.

1. Fill the skillet ¾ full of water and let it come to a boil. The skillet should hold at least 2 quarts of water. Add ½ teaspoon salt.

2. Hold plate of eggs in left hand. Take tablespoon in right hand, place the bottom of the spoon flat on the bottom of the skillet, and right in the center make a whirlpool in the water.

3. When the whirlpool is spinning rapidly (and *not* until then), slip the eggs directly into the middle of the whirlpool.

4. Place a lid on the skillet and *simmer* for from 2 to 3 minutes, depending on how soft you like the eggs.

5. Turn off the heat and cut the eggs apart.

6. Using the slotted lifter, lift the eggs, one at a time, from the water.

7. Hold bottom of lifter against a soft paper napkin to absorb all excess moisture.

8. Then place well-drained eggs on hot crisp toast or toasted rusks, well buttered. Serve *at once*.

The whirlpool swishes around and keeps the white portion in shape. The low heat and the covered water steam the eggs to the right tender quality. Start with one or two eggs; soon you will be able to do many this way.

Soft- and Hard-cooked Eggs

1. Bring the water in a saucepan to boiling point.

2. Reduce to simmering temperature and add eggs.

3. Cover and let stand 3 minutes for soft-cooked eggs, 8 minutes for medium, 25 minutes for hard-cooked.

4. Plunge hard-cooked eggs into cold water immediately.

5. Crack shells and start peeling at round end of egg. Holding eggs under running water helps to ease the shell off, leaving a smooth, unbroken surface of white.

Eggs in the shell may be cooked soft or hard, as pre-ferred. This emphasis on cooking eggs in water at *low temperature* is an example of the low-temperature rule that applies to all egg cookery. You can understand the importance of the rule when you remember that me-ringues, custards, Hollandaise sauce, soufflés, and omelets all depend upon eggs for their delicacy and lightness.

HOW-TO-DO BREAKFAST MEATS
Broiled Bacon

Broiling is cooking by dry, direct heat. The proper broil-ing of bacon is done by the same method as that required for the proper broiling of any other meat. Bacon, same as any other meat, may be pan-broiled or cooked in the broiler unit. Follow step-by-step directions carefully.

PAN-BROILED BACON

1. Place bacon strips in cold skillet.
2. Cook over moderate heat.
3. As fat accumulates in skillet, pour it off, holding bacon with pancake turner, or with lid.
4. Turn bacon as it browns and keep all fat poured off.
5. Don't *overcook,* for bacon should be delicately browned, evenly cooked, and crisp.
6. Remove from heat as soon as it's done and drain on soft paper toweling.
7. Serve on heated plates.

BACON IN BROILER UNIT

1. Place bacon strips close together on broiler rack.

2. Set 3 inches below electric unit, or below tip of blue flame.
3. Broil until lightly crisped and brown.
4. Turn and finish broiling.
5. Remove to drain on paper toweling.
6. Serve on heated plate.

Broiled Smoked Ham

1. Buy a thick slice—1½ inches—of smoked ham.
2. Gash fat edge with sharp knife, so it will not curl, but stay flat.
3. Holding fat edge against hot broiler rack, brush it lightly with fat.
4. Place ham on broiler rack about 3 inches from unit or blue flame.
5. Broil 6 or 8 minutes and turn.
6. Continue broiling 10 minutes more. Serve on heated platter.

Serves 3 to 4.

If you pan-broil this ham, follow basic HOW-TO-DO for bacon (page 52).

Frizzled Ham

1. Buy paper-thin slices of boiled ham.
2. Brush hot skillet with ham or bacon drippings, or with butter.
3. Pan-broil quickly until edges curl and frizzle and cook crisp.

4. Remove to hot platter and eat with your fingers.

Red-eye Gravy

1. After ham is pan-fried, take it up to serve on heated plate.
2. Let the small amount of fat in the skillet get very hot. Scrape all browned portion loose and quickly dash ¼ cup hot water into skillet. Stir a second or two and pour over ham in hot plate.

   Lickin' good on hot biscuits.

Canadian Bacon

Pan-broiling is best for Canadian bacon, as it has so little fat on it.

1. Heat heavy skillet and brush surface with bacon fat.
2. Broil the Canadian bacon quickly on one side.
3. Pour off accumulated fat and quickly broil other side.
4. Place on soft paper toweling to drain a minute.
5. Serve on heated plate.

SAUSAGE

1 pound link sausage
2 tablespoons water

1. Place link sausage in a cold skillet and sprinkle with 2 tablespoons water.
2. Cover with lid and cook over medium heat for 5 minutes.
3. Remove lid and pour off all fat and water.

4. Continue cooking, turning sausages gently so that they will not break through the tender skins. Cook slowly and turn as they brown.

5. As even a few drops of fat accumulate, be sure to pour off this fat.

6. When done, remove to soft paper toweling so that all excess fat is absorbed and serve from a heated platter.

Serves 4.

Unless fat is removed, the sausages will *fry* instead of *broil*. They should brown and be juicy and puffy in from 11 to 15 minutes, depending on the size of your skillet and the quality of your meat.

Frizzled Dried Beef

I keep dried beef in my refrigerator just as I do butter. Buy it by the half pound, sliced paper thin. Wrap it in aluminum foil and you have unlimited solutions to menu problems, emergencies, and the day nothing seems to taste just right for breakfast. It should be strictly against the law to soak this delightful meat in water, removing all flavor and ruining the quality. Also, I'm in favor of an investigation if it's served only in "white sauce."

Coat the surface of a heavy skillet with sweet butter and heat till it bubbles, but do not let the butter brown or scorch. Add the thin slices of dried beef and cook quickly until they curl and frizzle all around the edges. Remove to heated plate and serve piping hot. Mighty good with fried mush.

CODFISH CAKES

You will need:

½ pound salt codfish	Pepper to taste
4 medium-sized potatoes	1 tablespoon butter
½ teaspoon salt	1 egg, well beaten

Deep fat for frying

1. Separate salt codfish into flakes and cover with cold water.
2. Let this come to a boil, pour off water, and again cover with fresh cold water.
3. Just as soon as it comes to a boil, turn the heat down to low, put a tight lid on, and simmer until codfish is moist and tender (about 25 minutes).
4. Pare and cook potatoes, mash, and beat until fluffy. When light and smooth, add salt, plenty of pepper, butter, and egg.
5. Drain cooked codfish well and stir it into the hot mashed potatoes.
6. Shape into flat cakes or into cylinder shapes and roll lightly in flour.
7. Fry in deep hot fat, about 375 degrees, for about 4 to 6 minutes. Drain on soft paper and serve hot.

Serves about 4.

HOW-TO-DO CEREALS

Table for Cereals

CEREAL	WATER	AMOUNT IT YIELDS
1 cup corn meal	5-6 cups	5 cups
1 cup rolled oats	2 cups	2 cups
1 cup whole-wheat cereal	5-6 cups	3 cups
1 cup rice	2 cups	3 cups

Allow ½ teaspoon salt to each quart of water used.

Oatmeal

1. Allow 2 cups of water to 1 cup of oatmeal.
2. Place in top of double boiler over boiling water and cook 30 minutes. Do this as you are preparing dinner.
3. Pour into buttered custard cups and set in refrigerator overnight.
4. While you are getting breakfast, just set cups in a shallow pan of hot water and heat on top of range or in oven. By the time breakfast is ready the oatmeal will be piping hot. Heat attractive bowls, too.
5. Turn the oatmeal molds out into hot dishes, add a dot of butter and a sprinkling of brown sugar.
6. Beside each hot mold of oatmeal add a serving of tart applesauce, or 2 peeled canned apricots, or add plumped raisins, prunes, or dates.
7. Over all pour rich cream.
   Serves 3.

My experience has been that these *small* servings of oatmeal, all dressed up, invariably call for second helpings. Be sure the oatmeal is well cooked, hot, and attractively served—and don't talk about it.

CORN MEAL MUSH . . . AS CEREAL

You will need:

1 cup corn meal, yellow or white	½ teaspoon salt
	1 cup cold milk
3 cups boiling water	

1. Measure corn meal and salt into heavy saucepan.
2. Stir in milk.

3. Stir in boiling water.

4. Place over moderately high heat and, using wooden spoon, stir carefully every minute until bubbles shoot up all over surface of mush.

5. Now cover with good tight lid, reduce heat to low, and simmer for 45 minutes.

6. Remove the lid last 15 minutes and let mush cook very dry. Note that 1 cup corn meal has now expanded into about 3 cups of corn-meal mush.

7. Serve hot as a porridge with milk or cream and with sugar. Or serve with butter and sugar. Sugar mixed with cinnamon is often a favorite topping.

Serves 6 to 8.

NOTE: This porridge is a base for crusty fried mush, or for a tamale pie (page 96).

CRUSTY FRIED MUSH

You will need:

> 1 recipe corn-meal mush (page 57)
> Fat to fry

1. Prepare corn-meal mush.

2. Turn into well-buttered loaf pan and put aside to become cold and to set. Requires several hours or overnight.

3. Remove from pan and pat perfectly dry with paper napkin. Then cut into pieces about as long as your finger and 1/3 as wide.

4. Drop into deep hot fat about 370 degrees and fry

golden brown and crusty. Drain on heated cake rack
and serve hot.

Serves 6 to 8.

Or, if you want thin slices, cut thin and dip into meal
and fry in skillet with half bacon or ham drippings and
shortening. Use only enough fat to prevent burning, and
keep heat moderate.

FRIED HOMINY GRITS

You will need:

1 cup hominy grits	½ teaspoon salt
4 cups rapidly boiling water	Butter or other fat for pan frying

1. Stir grits slowly into rapidly boiling water, stirring
   well.
2. Add salt. Cook slowly, covered, for about 45 minutes.
   Stir frequently. Remove lid last 10 minutes of cooking.
3. Turn into well-oiled loaf pan and cool overnight.
4. When set and cold, slice in thick portions.
5. Fry in hot butter or other fat until golden brown.
6. Serve with Red-eye Gravy (see page 54), honey, or
   any jam or jelly.

Serves 4 to 6.

GAY BREAKFASTS

Just any old reason, or none at all, may set off a gay breakfast. One time I did a whole series of Sunday-night suppers just because someone gave me a clever little Koa
Wood nutmeg grinder. Of course I had to go out and

buy an extravagant lemon-colored French-pottery set
from which I served blissful green pea soup. But that
wee grating of fresh nutmeg on top of my soup was worth
remembering long after I forgot the cost of the pottery.

Gay Breakfast 1

Strawberries and Pineapple Spears (page 174)
Poached Eggs on Hot Rusks (page 50)
Sautéed Chicken Livers (page 258) and
Grilled Canadian Bacon (page 54)
Popovers and Wild Plum Jelly (page 45)
Coffee—and More Coffee

Gay Breakfast 2

Big Pitcher Icy Cold Apricot Nectar with Thin Lime Slices
Miniature Egg Cutlets (page 237)
Broiled Ham (page 53)
Assorted Sweet Rolls, Heated and Buttered
Coffee

Some of this breakfast gaiety will be because your table
simply sings. A crisp clean cloth, shining glasses, gleam-
ing silver, and pretty dishes, with even a few flowers, set
the mood.   *   *   *

Hot-weather Menus

"Naw—no breakfast for me, it's too Hot to eat!" That's
regular for midsummer and not peculiar to your flock
at all. Have your answers ready. Here are some of mine.

1.   Frosty Pitcher of Ice Cold Apricot Nectar and
Orange Juice Mixed
Hot Toasted Buttered English Muffins (page 47)
Spread with Thick Layer of Plum Jam or Preserves
Iced Coffee

2. Big Bowl Ripe Blackberries and Cream
Popovers (page 45)
and Red Currant Jelly
Lots of Frizzled Dried Beef (page 55)
Iced Coffee (half and half milk and strong coffee)

3. Cantaloupe Halves
Scrambled Eggs with Bits of Bacon (page 49)
Golden Brown Crisp Fried Mush (page 57)
Blackberry Jam
Iced Coffee

The Breakfast You Are Famous For

Maybe you've established yourself as famous for many breakfasts. But for my new homemakers, these old, tried breakfasts of mine are good starters to master and to vary.

FAMOUS BREAKFAST 1

Honey Dew Melon with Lime Wedges
Waffles (page 44)
Pot of Blackberry Jam   Jug of Honey   Pitcher Maple Sirup
Canadian Bacon and Plain Bacon
Poached Eggs (page 50)
Large Cups of Coffee

I always break crisp waffles in 4 sections. Serve the first "go around" of poached eggs and plain bacon and 2 hot buttered waffle sections. Then bring clean heated plates, a tray of Canadian bacon, and waffle iron to the table. From there on, serve waffles off the hot iron, with a little kettle full of melted butter and all the jam, honey, and sirup you want. I usually add broken pecans to the last waffle and make more coffee.

FAMOUS BREAKFAST 2

Ripe Peaches and Cream
Scrambled Eggs (page 49). Frizzled Chipped Beef (page 55)
and Broiled Tomatoes
Hot Biscuits and Pear Honey (page 263)
Iced Coffee

FAMOUS BREAKFAST 3

Chilled Blueberries Dusted with Powdered Sugar
Omelet (page 227)
Grilled Tomato Slices
Tiny Hot Orange Biscuits (page 40)
Pot Fragrant Hot Tea (page 250)

Easy Tray Breakfasts

A tray breakfast may go to the porch on a leisurely day,
or it can be carried to the bedroom to be eaten in peace
and quiet when morning planning is essential. There are
any number of reasons that make an excuse for tray
breakfasts.

1
Large Glass Orange Juice
Cooked Cereal (page 56)
with Raisins and Dates
Brown Sugar or Honey
Real Cream
Toasted Hot Doughnuts
Coffee

2
Fruit or Melon in Season
Thin Ham Slice and Fried Egg in Individual Skillet (pages 53, 48)
Toasted Buns, Buttered
Strawberry Preserves
Coffee

3
Pineapple Chunks
Double-boiler Scrambled Eggs (page 49)
and
Crisp Brown Sausage Patties
Hot Cinnamon Rolls

Economy Breakfast Menus

Comes the last of the month and you've overstepped with the grocery money. No quickly done bacon and eggs for a few days. But what can you plan when there's not enough in the budget for eggs and bacon? Well, you can still make breakfast interesting, nourishing, and different —and above all things don't mention *why*.

ECONOMY BREAKFAST 1

Frosted Prune Juice with Lemon Slice
Small Omelets (page 227)
Big Bowl Applesauce or My Baked Rhubarb (page 174)
All Bran Muffins

ECONOMY BREAKFAST 2

Grapefruit Juice
Hot Cakes (page 43)
with Honey
End Slices Ham Grilled (page 53)
Coffee

ECONOMY BREAKFAST 3

Pineapple Juice (or fresh fruit in season)
Oatmeal (page 57)
Hot Buttered Toast
Tart Jam or Jelly
Coffee

3. Dinner

Some people think that when one says "HOW-TO-DO A DINNER" it should mean a party dinner, a company dinner. Nothing of the sort. The important dinners of our lives are the family dinners, the dinner concoctions and combinations that just hit the fancy of our beloved home folks.

As a matter of fact, it is a good idea for inexperienced homemakers to make it a rule to treat company to their _simple_ dishes—good dishes, good food, of course, but always the ones they know backward and forward, ones they _know_ will come out right and stay right, even when guests are late.

As for the family—they are the ones who deserve the special effort. For them one can do all kinds of things— take time to perfect some more complicated favorites (who cares if they aren't just so at first—a gal has to learn). Dishes that require an eagle eye up to the last moment are also family affairs. "Hey, get your hands washed and get to the table; here I come!"

Getting right down to brass tacks, I honestly believe that each new homemaker can soon master basic recipes. When you have actually perfected these basic How-to-do's it is easy to add a few frills: set a pretty table, plan a thoughtfully appropriate menu, and even give a dinner party!

If you have mastered basic meat cookery, basic egg cookery, and a few other How-to-do's there will be an ease about preparing dinner which will make you feel gay. If you have planned, as directed in the dinner pattern (page 71), there will be a sense of satisfaction about the accomplishment of a successful dinner which will make you happy and gay too.

You see why a thoughtful approach to meal planning is important. Learning how-to-do and really taking time to perfect recipes for dinner bubbles over to guests and to your family when you prepare a perfect dinner.

IT IS A GREAT HELP TO HAVE EMERGENCY SUPPLIES

Remember the neighbor who always had all the answers when company came unannounced? She was poised because she had planned. This could be you, if you build up a reserve supply of canned and dried foods in your emergency cupboard, and then keep it filled.

If you are lucky and have a home freezer, that's the end of emergencies, for it holds menus galore ready to serve.

Maybe you will start with a shelf, but try to make this space grow each week. Watch sales and save up for specials. Always replace each item used and don't borrow from the shelf, unless there *is* an emergency.

HERE IS A LIST OF "MUSTS":

Peach Halves
Whole Apricots
Big Black Cherries
Pineapple Circles
Whole Figs
Green Gage Plums
Cranberry Sauce
Sour Cherries (red)
Applesauce

Mushroom Soup
Tomato Soup
Vegetable Soup
Clam Chowder
Chicken Soup
Chicken Broth
Dehydrated Soups

Mayonnaise
Dessert Sauces
Spaghetti Sauces

Relishes
Ripe Olives
Pimientos
Green Olives

Rusks
Biscuit Mix
Gingerbread Mix
Cake Mixes
Pudding Mix

Minced Clams
Salmon
Tuna Fish
Shrimp
Crab
Lobster

Whole Kernel Corn
Asparagus
String Beans
Pork and Beans
Hominy
Limas
Peas
Mushrooms

Anchovy Paste
Jar of Grated Cheese
Sherry Wine

Jars of Dried Chipped
   Beef
Jars of Chicken
Baked Ham
Corned Beef Hash
Chili
Tamales
Ravioli

Fine Noodles
Powdered Milk
Rice

THE LANGUAGE OF COOKING

There is a cooking vocabulary which everyone must be familiar with in order to make the best use of modern recipes. In every cookbook you meet such directions as braise, poach, sauté, roast, deep-fry, and many others. It is well to brush up occasionally on this language of cooking.

You will notice that I'm a plain nagger on simmering, on LOW heat, and on gentle cooking. The good tight lid gets a continuous workout and I'm anti-boil with most food. Braising is one of my pet projects and I do poach a mean egg. To sauté is not to fry. Also, there is no mystery about these terms. Actually they are descriptive of basic methods we thoroughly master.

To *simmer*—To cook below boiling. The heat must be LOW.

To *braise*—To cook by slow, moist cooking for a long period of time. Always use a good tight lid. All less tender cuts of meat are braised, either on top of range or in the oven.

To *sauté*—To cook in very small amount of fat over gentle heat. Sauté onions, mushrooms, and the like.

To *poach*—To cook covered in water at LOW temperature. Poach eggs and fish.

To *deep-fry*—To fry in deep fat at even temperature, usually moderately high. A cube of bread browns in one minute at 375 degrees. This is the temperature used for many foods such as doughnuts and fritters. Deep-frying is the best frying method, for less fat is absorbed in this method.

To *roast*—To cook by dry direct heat, period! No water is added. No lid is used.

It's a mighty good plan to memorize the definitions for roasting and braising. When you go into your meat market, you then know the way to cook all the meat you see. Roast more tender cuts of meat. Braise less tender cuts of meat. That's all.

To *gash fat*—To cut all the way through fat around a chop, steak, or thick slice of ham. Cut from outside edge just to the lean meat, so that the fat will spread and be flat on the broiler as it cooks. Otherwise the meat buckles as it heats.

To *sear*—To brown quickly, usually meat. Searing holds juices inside the meat.

To *shred*—To cut in fine shreds on a grater. Shred cabbage, cheese, and peppers.

To *boil water*—Well, you'd be surprised that many beginners (and others) do not really boil water. They just think they do. Water is not boiling when steam forms, or when bubbles show on the bottom. Boiling is 212 degrees and at that temperature the bubbles dance up on top of the water and break through. That's boiling.

To *dredge in flour*—To roll in flour till lightly and evenly coated. Dredge raisins, nuts, and fruits for batters, so that they do not sink to the bottom. Always save out a little flour from a recipe for this, so that extra flour need not be added.

To *broil*—To cook by dry direct heat. *For example:* Place a thick steak or chop on broiler rack just below heat and cook on each side, at high temperature, till done. Or *pan-broil*—To cook on very hot skillet, pouring off all fat.

HOW-TO-DO A DINNER MENU

When you sit down to plan dinner menus you don't just get settled and chew a pencil while you try to figure out what to have from soup to nuts. That is a terrible way to plan a menu.

Start out by thinking up family favorites that you like to serve. Maybe it's a cherry pie for one dinner; you haven't made one in a long time. For another dinner there could be that elegant minced-clam soup as a starting point (if you haven't heard about *my* minced-clam soup, do, please, turn quickly to page 108. You are missing something!) It may also be braised pork chops. It *could* be anything!

Once you have the starting point for a dinner menu, it almost begins to plan itself. Possibly braised pork chops suggest an accompaniment of apple rings (see my recipe, page 173. I can recommend it highly). Brown rice or a baked potato could go with this. A tossed salad takes care of raw and green food. Then you say to yourself, "Well, after such a dinner, I'd better go light on the dessert." You think of a half grapefruit, or lemon or orange sherbet, but if your family appetites can take it, up comes the favorite, lemon meringue pie.

See what I mean about menu making? Just for fun

let us have a look at the menu after it is finished and see what it gives the family in terms of:

1. Food (nutrition)
2. Color (to appeal to the appetite)
3. Texture of food (to make it taste good)

1. *Food.* There you have ... meat

> potatoes or brown rice
> salad green
> fruit (cooked in pie filling
>   or in sherbet
> bread—butter

Just one vegetable (aside from salad) ... how about adding some buttered broccoli?

Is there sufficient raw food?
How about starting with half a grapefruit?

2. *Color.* Good brown of meat—potatoes—rice.

Green salad (let's add some carrot sticks for the orange color).

Yellow of sherbet or pie.

3. *Texture* of food. (Do you ever stop to think of texture when you are planning meals? Is the food all soft? Is it all "soupy"? Is it all made up of dry dishes without sauces? A meal that consists of any one of these, exclusively, is one that you cannot enjoy.)

In this menu, with soft pork, the brown rice would be of better texture than (let us say) mashed potatoes. A crisp salad green picks up the texture, too.

Menu Making Pattern

Now then here it is—all tied up in a neat little package.

I. Include at least one of these in your daily main meal:

> meat   cheese
> fowl   eggs
> fish   dried beans or dried peas

II. Include potatoes, unless menu has macaroni, rice, or dried beans.

III. Select a cooked vegetable, yellow or leafy green, or both.

IV. Breads and rolls (whole-grain are best, but, if white, do be sure the bread is enriched). Butter or margarine.

V. Remember fruit, ice cream, custards, puddings, when deciding on dessert.

VI. Beverage may be coffee, tea, or milk—but remember, a minimum of 1 pint milk daily for each adult and 1 quart for children.

Dinner Design Based on Menu Pattern

Wedge of Melon
Ham Loaf with Pineapple Slices
or
Braised Pork Chops with Red Apple Circles
Baked Potatoes (page 151)
Buttered Broccoli
Wedge Crisp Romaine with French Dressing
Lemon Meringue Pie (pages 182, 183)
Coffee, Tea, or Milk

DINNER MENU FAVORITES

You might be interested to know what recipes of mine
have been favorites with my family and friends. Many
times through every year I made my white coconut cake
and my angel-food cake with orange glaze for my dad.
Sometimes I varied the white cake by using caramel icing
(page 103), or my lemon filling (page 192) and for him I
always grated fresh coconut and piled it on deep.

Dad always declared the cake he was eating was the
best and never failed to predict that I could make a for-
tune on those cakes, together with my white fruit cake,
Aunt Bill's Brown Candy, and Aunt Susan's Orange
Mint.

These are among the most popular recipes tested and
approved by thousands of homemakers for many thousands of menus.

My husband says he casts his vote for my ham loaf,
tamale pie, and corn pudding and that I get a "special
scald" on lemon meringue pie. I don't argue this with
him; you know lemon pie (pages 182, 183) is never
scalded, don't you? He specially likes baked or fried
guinea and my Long Island duck with orange, and he
says he thinks my brand of macaroni and cheese and corn-
bread are among the best servings I offer him.

My homemaker friends never fail to list as their favorites the recipes I have given them for turkey stuffing, corn
soup, strawberry preserves, and Red Earth Cake.

Among the How-to-do's which follow I hope there are
many dishes you will adopt as prime favorites in your
own household. There are lots of dinnertime recipes I
don't want you to miss.

Let me urge you to use the Index of this book daily. That's the easy way to find what you want.

We'd better roll up our sleeves at this point and get busy.

My Family's Favorite Menu

Braised Rump "Roast"
Rich Velvety Brown Gravy
Browned Crusty Potatoes
Wedges Lettuce with Cardinal Dressing
Pascal Celery
My Hot Bread Trick
Frozen Orange Juice Ice Cream
Pineapple Drop Cookies
Coffee

WORK SHEET

GROCERY LIST

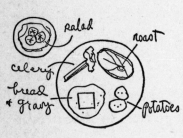

4½ pounds beef rump (with suet)
V-8 Cocktail juice
celery
parsley
carrots
onion
frozen orange juice
heavy cream
lemons

HOW-TO-DO

1. Prepare rump "roast" and put into oven
2. Make frozen-orange-juice ice cream
3. Make cardinal dressing
4. Prepare potatoes
5. Prepare lettuce
6. Prepare rolls
7. Prepare coffee
8. Make gravy

The meat should cook approximately 3 hours.

As soon as you have the meat in the oven, make the ice cream. Keep in the freezing unit.

Cardinal Dressing may be kept indefinitely.

Make gravy last, as rolls heat.

Place dessert bowl in refrigerator to chill for ice cream.

HOW-TO-DO BRAISED BEEF RUMP

Buy a 4½-pound beef rump. This is all meat, without a vestige of waste. There is no bone, no gristle, no extra fat.

You will need:

4½-pound rump roast of beef (with suet)	3 sprigs parsley
1 cup V-8 Cocktail juice (or tomato juice)	2 carrots, chopped
	A few peppercorns (whole pepper)
2 stalks celery and leaves	½ teaspoon salt
1 medium onion, quartered	

4-6 medium-sized potatoes, pared

1. Heat a small roaster very hot.

2. Rub surface with small piece of the beef suet, or fat.

3. Place meat flat on the hot roaster, so that it seals tightly to the roaster.

4. Sear and brown. Requires about three minutes.

5. Turn and brown on all sides, including fat side.

6. While sizzling hot add: V-8 Cocktail juice; sliced onion; chopped carrots; celery and leaves, cut fine; salt; black pepper from grinder.

7. Cover with tight-seal lid.

8. Place in 325-degree oven and braise for from 2½ hours to 3½ hours.

9. One hour before roast is done, add potatoes; cover roaster and continue cooking.

10. The meat should be so tender it may be cut with a fork. If not that done, continue cooking. But DON'T turn heat up. Time varies according to quality of meat. Very best beef requires about 2½ hours. As quality decreases, time increases.

Serves 8 to 10 (and for smaller family is a roast to be used for planned-overs, later in the week).

When you have mastered this basic recipe for braising, you know how-to-do all the less tender cuts of meat in your meat market. Just remember, BRAISING is LONG— SLOW—MOIST cookery. You'll have tender, delicious meat and heavenly gravy each time.

How-to-do Brown Gravy

1. Always make the gravy in roaster or pan in which meat cooked so that all browned particles and coating may be used, because this adds quality, flavor, and color to the gravy.

2. Remove meat to heated platter and keep warm.

3. Pour all fat and juice into a measuring cup. Fat will rise to the top.

4. Using a ladle, skim off fat, until you have ½ cup fat and juice left in the cup.

5. Pour this ½ cup back into the roaster and place over low heat.

6. Using a wooden spoon, scrape every bit of brown coating from sides and bottom of roaster, tilting roaster to keep it all at one end, over burner.

7. Now begin adding ½ cup flour, stirring it carefully into the fat. Add slowly and keep heat low. If this flour scorches, the gravy will not thicken.

8. When a smooth *emulsion* is formed by cooking and stirring the browned fat and juices together over low heat . . .

9. Then, add 4 cups of cold water. Add it gradually and stir rapidly, until no lumps appear.

10. After one or two cups of water are added, increase the heat to very high and stir thoroughly. Be sure to dig out every particle of brown as this gravy cooks. It will require only about 6 to 8 minutes after water is added.

11. Add salt, pepper, and a dash of tabasco. Taste for seasonings. Serve piping hot.

HOW-TO-DO CARDINAL DRESSING

½ cup sugar
2 teaspoons salt
2 teaspoons paprika
2 teaspoons ginger

2 teaspoons dry mustard
½ cup wine vinegar
4 tablespoons catsup
½ cup olive oil

1. Mix dry ingredients in small deep bowl.

2. Add catsup and vinegar and stir well.

3. Now add olive oil, a little at a time, beating constantly until a perfect emulsion is formed.

4. Store in a bottle and shake before using.

Makes 1⅓ cups.

This is a smooth, satiny dressing with an unusual lilt! It is delightful with fruit salad when the amount of sugar is doubled.

HOW-TO-DO WIN'S HOT BREAD TRICK

1. Using half a loaf of sliced bread, cut down through the stack of slices.
2. Now turn the slices so that all crusts are on the bottom and cut edge is up.
3. Run a couple of skewers into each end of the slices.
4. Brush the cut edge with softened butter.
5. Lay across a pan to fit the loaf and bake in a 400-degree oven about 10 to 12 minutes.
6. Serve hot in folded napkin. Slices are hot, buttery, and lightly toasted. Delicious! Add parsley, chives, or minced watercress to the butter, if you like.

This was first served to me in San Francisco. My hostess used whole-wheat bread, cut off all crusts, and sprinkled sesame seed generously over the slices before toasting.

It was passed with the first course—cold jellied Madrilene. This was years ago and I can still recall everything about that supper.

Remind yourself to serve menus worth remembering.

HOW-TO-DO FROZEN ORANGE JUICE
ICE CREAM

This is an original recipe. I stirred this up for a guest who could eat no sugar. The whole family enjoyed it so much that it is repeated frequently. It is a dessert that will keep almost indefinitely in your refrigerator tray.

1. Beat two egg whites very stiff.
2. In a second bowl, beat one cup of whipping cream, not too stiff.
3. Gently fold the cream into the egg whites.
4. Then fold into the egg whites and cream one whole can concentrated frozen orange juice.
5. Add two teaspoons kirsch, if you like.
6. Turn into refrigerator tray and freeze until mushy.
7. Then whip lightly with wire whisk and return to refrigerator to continue freezing.

Serves six.

HOW-TO-DO PINEAPPLE DROP COOKIES

These are delicious light cookies having a crusty thin edge and flavorful bites of juicy pineapple through them. Easiest cooky I ever made, too.

⅓ cup butter or margarine	1 cup flour (all-purpose)
½ cup sugar	¼ teaspoon soda
1 egg	¼ cup crushed pineapple
2 tablespoons hot water	

1. Cream butter and sugar together until fluffy. It is important to get this mixture really puffy and perfectly light, so beat lots of air into it.
2. Sift flour and soda together and add a little flour to the butter mixture (about 3 tablespoons).
3. Next, add the well-beaten egg and mix.

4. Then add flour and pineapple alternately.

5. Last, dash in 2 tablespoons hot, not boiling, water and beat well.

6. Drop by teaspoons onto lightly oiled cooky sheet. Leave plenty of space between them, as they spread. This is a drop batter that forms a definite lump when dropped from the spoon.

7. Bake in 375-degree oven, 10 to 12 minutes.

8. Then place on wire cake cooler. They should not be stacked.

If pineapple is very juicy, some of the juice should be drained off, as you need much more pineapple than juice.

NOTE: They should not be placed in cake box or cooky jar as they'll stick together. Keep on wire cake cooler, or between sheets of waxed paper. Really no difficulty about storing, for they never last long enough to prove a problem!

COMPANY MENUS

My Ham Loaf
Southern Corn Pudding
Buttered Broccoli
Hot Butterfly Rolls with Chive Butter
Romaine Wedges with Roquefort Dressing
Apple Dumplings with Orange Pastry
Coffee

How-to-do Your Company Dinner

First write out your menu.

Next draw a sketch of a plate arranged to pass to your guests.

EXAMPLE

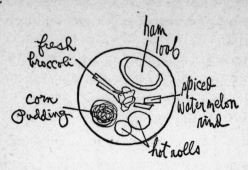

This visualizes the dinner for you. Quickly jot down a list of extra serving dishes, spoons, forks, bread baskets, or other table needs which will be required. Maybe they are on high shelves, in drawers, or need polishing. Before you forget, collect all linen, china, and other table equipment and see that it is ready to use.

Next, check ingredients for each recipe and make a complete list of all grocery needs. As you are doing this, also check the pans, casserole dishes, and preparation tools to be sure nothing is missing. (Don't wait till you are ready to pour the corn pudding into your pet baking dish and find it was left at the last PTA dinner.)

Until you are accustomed to doing company dinners, let me urge you to plan carefully. Always try out recipes on your family first. Don't experiment with a recipe for your company menu. It might be perfect, but be sure it's your own recipe before sharing it. I used always to do a dress rehearsal on my dinners, without cooked food of course, the night before. It was good to set the table late at night, with no interruptions, and arrange all the serving dishes and tools to insure a smooth production.

Suddenly I discovered that I had no lump sugar, or the pepper grinder was empty, or there wasn't room for my flowers, or I felt stuffy in the dress I'd planned to wear. So I had time to fix everything right. It was always fun to revise some detail to please my family as they put in their suggestions. And it invariably gave me a sense of poise, which made me enjoy the dinner party and the dinner. Try it!

WORK SHEET

GROCERY LIST

¾ lb. ham (smoked)
½ lb. veal
1 lb. beef
spiced watermelon rind
whole kernel corn
broccoli
V-8 Cocktail juice
rusks
butter
milk and heavy cream

LIST FOR ME

get candles
get lump sugar
get new pot chives
clean silver
check table mats
check chop plate
get new powder puffs
and guest soap!
have TV set fixed!

NOW, IN THIS ORDER

1. Make apple dumplings and bake them.
2. Prepare ham loaf.
3. Prepare corn pudding.
4. Prepare broccoli.
5. Prepare romaine.
6. Make Roquefort dressing.
7. Prepare rolls.
8. Prepare coffee.

For the young homemaker, who says she always has trouble getting everything done at the same time, this *preparation order* will help you. It means that you might even start early in the morning and prepare each serving, then *cook* them the last hour before dinner. And you will follow the same order of preparation, if you have only an hour or two before dinner.

The ham loaf bakes at 350 degrees for 1 hour.

The corn pudding bakes at 350 degrees for ½ hour. Put the ham loaf in to bake and by the time your corn pudding is *prepared* it may share the oven for that last 30 minutes. The broccoli requires only 20 minutes, but, when drained well, it may wait with safety for seasonings and last-minute heating.

Romaine is always especially easy to clean, keep crisp, and prepare. French dressing blended with crumbled Roquefort is a quickie. *Prepare* the rolls and coffee in any spare 5 minutes.

ENCOURAGEMENT DEPARTMENT FOR MY NEW HOMEMAKERS

IF DINNER MUST WAIT:

Cover the ham loaf with aluminum foil.

Cover the corn pudding with aluminum foil, not touching top of pudding, and set the casserole in a shallow pan of hot water.

Put them into a warm oven and leave the oven door partly open.

Set the rolls in also, and even the broccoli, in a tightly covered baking dish.

Never finish salad till ready to serve.

HOW-TO-DO MY HAM LOAF

You will need:

1 pound beef
¾ pound smoked ham (not fresh pork)
½ pound veal
1 teaspoon each mustard (dry), salt, pepper, and paprika
1 egg

1½ cups V-8 Cocktail, or tomato juice
1 cup dry crumbs, finely powdered
½ clove garlic, finely minced (or 1 tablespoon diced onion, sautéed)

Buy good quality beef, veal, and smoked ham. Ask your meat man to grind them together with coarsest blade. End pieces of ham may be used, but do not substitute fresh pork.

1. Mix all dry seasonings with slightly beaten egg, stirring well.

2. Add V-8 Cocktail juice (or tomato juice) and stir.

3. Add finely powdered bread crumbs to meat, mixing lightly.

4. Stir in egg, juice, and seasonings. The secret of this ham loaf lies in the fact that it is mixed VERY LIGHTLY. *Do not mash* or *squeeze* or *overstir*. Pat it gently into shape in a shallow pan approximately 7½ inches by 11 inches and not more than 2 inches deep. Sprinkle lightly on top with finely powdered crumbs and pour 1/3 cup of tomato juice around the loaf (do not pour juice over the loaf). Bake uncovered in 350-degree oven, one hour.

Serves 6 to 8.

HOW-TO-DO SOUTHERN CORN PUDDING

From a hot baking dish serve old-fashioned Southern Corn Pudding. Whole grains of yellow corn in quivery custard flecked with strips of pimiento and green pepper under a satiny light beige topping . . .

You will need:

1 egg, well beaten	1 tablespoon flour
½ teaspoon salt	1 tablespoon butter, melted
⅛ teaspoon pepper	1 cup milk
¼ teaspoon paprika	1 can whole kernel corn
¼ teaspoon dry mustard	1 pimiento (canned)
1 green pepper	

1. In mixing bowl beat 1 egg until light and foamy.

2. Add ½ teaspoon salt, ⅛ teaspoon pepper, ¼ teaspoon paprika, ¼ teaspoon dry mustard, and 1 tablespoon flour.

3. Stir in 1 tablespoon melted butter and 1 cup milk.

4. Add 1 can whole-kernel corn.

5. Using scissors, cut 1 pimiento (canned) into strips and cut 1 green pepper into shreds and stir through mixture.

6. Turn into well-buttered *shallow* baking dish, 1-quart size at least—and shallow, as you need plenty of surface.

7. Bake 30 minutes in 350-degree oven.

Serves 4.

HOW-TO-DO ROQUEFORT DRESSING

½ cup olive oil
4 tablespoons lemon juice
Dash salt

½ teaspoon dry mustard
1 teaspoon paprika
½ teaspoon sugar

¼ pound grated Roquefort cheese

Measure ingredients into a jar and shake hard until dressing is smooth. When just ready to serve, add to crisp wedges of lettuce or romaine.

Makes about ¾ cup.

HOW-TO-DO APPLE DUMPLINGS WITH ORANGE PASTRY

1. Core and peel 6 tart, juicy apples.

2. Add 1½ cups water to the peelings and cores and cook until mushy.

3. Strain juice and add 1 cup sugar to it and cook 10 minutes. It is thin.

4. Remove and add red food coloring to give a deep rich color.

5. Roll orange pastry as for piecrust (see below). Cut into 3-inch strips, just long enough to wrap around apple.

6. Fit strip around apple, sealing tightly. Be sure to cover the bottom with dough.

7. Place apples in shallow baking dish so they do not touch.

8. Fill center of each apple with sugar.

9. Top each apple with a dash of nutmeg and a dot of butter and pour juice around (not over) the apples.

10. Bake in moderate oven, 350 degrees, for one hour. Serve warm with cream.

HOW TO MAKE ORANGE PASTRY

1 cup flour
¼ teaspoon salt
½ teaspoon grated orange rind

⅓ cup shortening
4 tablespoons chilled, strained orange juice

1. Mix flour with salt and grated rind.
2. Cut in shortening, using pastry blender, until mixture is like coarse meal.
3. Using fork, mix in the orange juice, tossing mixture up from bottom of bowl.
4. Pour out on sheet of waxed paper and with about three pressures of hands from outside form pastry into ball.
5. Roll about ⅛ inch thick on cloth-covered board, lightly floured.
6. Use as directed in step number 5 above.

Serves 6.

*   *   *

HOW-TO-DO
CHICKEN CHOW MEIN FOR A PARTY

This is a beautiful serving and so good for large groups. Most of the preparation may be done early in the day and assembled at serving time. Much to your surprise it is very economical menu material.

One of my favorite buffet suppers is

Chilled Honey Dew Melon or Cantaloupe
Chicken Chow Mein
A Tray Filled with
Poached Fruit or Drifts of Raspberry and Lemon Sherbet
Almond Wafers
Hot Tea

1. Simmer a 3- to 4-pound fat hen or fowl until tender and let it cool in its own well-seasoned broth.

2. Remove meat from bones but keep breast all in one piece.

3. Cut all but breast in good bite-size pieces and moisten with chicken broth.

4. Measure 2½ cups broth or stock in which chicken is cooked.

5. Cook 2 cups rice perfectly—grains stand apart white and fluffy (page 149). (Steps 1 through 5 may even be done the day before your dinner party.)

6. Where Chinese markets are available Chinese vegetables are available. Or if you buy LaChoy Chinese canned vegetables and sauce you'll be pleased with your results.

7. In addition to chicken, broth, and rice *you will need:*

2 cans hot toasted noodles
½ cup water chestnuts
½ cup bamboo shoots
1 cup Chinese bean sprouts
1 cup mushrooms
1 cup celery, cut fine
3 tablespoons soy sauce
1 medium onion, diced

¼ pound blanched almonds, toasted
1 bunch young green onions, or scallions
Ripe olives and radishes
The largest platter or chop plate you have

8. In heavy saucepan, simmer water chestnuts, bamboo shoots, sprouts, mushrooms, and celery with 1½ cups chicken stock for 10 minutes.

9. In large skillet, melt 3 tablespoons of butter and sauté the onion until soft and yellow. Add 1 tablespoon flour and 1 teaspoon salt and blend thoroughly over low heat.

10. When well cooked, add 1 cup chicken stock and cook, stirring to make smooth sauce. Add soy sauce and stir well.

11. Now add all the vegetables and stir together lightly. Keep very hot till ready to serve.

12. Use largest platter. Cover center with mound of hot rice.

13. Over this pour the chow mein, vegetables, and sauce.

14. Around the edge pour a row of the hot toasted noodles.

15. Across the top, over all, arrange in an orderly row the shredded scallions or green onions. I use one of those bean-shredder gadgets to sliver them lengthwise, using several inches of green tops. They are very fine and most attractive.

16. On top of them place long strips of moist chicken breast.

17. Strew toasted almonds generously over chicken breast.

18. Garnish at each end with crisp red radishes and big black ripe olives.

Somehow get this production to the table piping hot and serve it with fanfare. It's really not a lot of trouble and is so very good to eat.

Serves 8.

More Company Menus

MENU 1

Broiled Chicken Halves (page 141)
Garnished with Pickled Peaches and Spiced Watermelon Rind
Deep Glass Bowl Filled with Crushed Ice in Which Are Buried
Radishes, Ripe Olives, Celery Hearts, Finochio (Anise)
Volcano Potatoes (page 236)
Little Yellow Squash in Paprika Butter (page 153)
Chilled Pineapple Chunks with Kirsch
or
Fresh Strawberries with Port Wine
Small Black Coffee

MENU 2

Hot Spiced Tomato Bouillon
My Chicken Chow Mein (page 87)
Fruit Bowl of
Peeled Apricots and Green Gage Plums with Bits of
Candied Ginger
Pineapple Drop Cookies (page 78)   Hot Tea

MENU 3

Long Island Duck with Orange Sauce (page 141)
Wild Rice
Green Asparagus
Hot Toasted Sesame Seed Rolls
Fresh Fruit Salad
Raspberry Ice and Angel Food Cake (page 198)
Iced Coffee

More Favorite Menus

MENU 1

Chicken and Dumplings (pages 94, 95)
Red Cabbage Slaw in Cabbage Head (pages 100, 101)
Baked Custard (page 105)
Hot Gingerbread (page 106)
Coffee

MENU 2

Susan's Own Vegetable Soup (page 93)
Hot Corn Bread Squares
Pascal Celery
Carrot Sticks with Celery Salt
Warm Apple Pie (page 105) and Cheese
Pot of Hot Tea

MENU 3

Barbecued Spare Ribs (page 95)
Baked Yams   Broiled Tomatoes
Hot Garlic Rye Bread
Dill Pickles   Bermuda Onion Rings
Rosy Baked Apples, Glazed (page 104)
Coffee

MENU 4

Jellied Consommé with Thin Lemon Slice
Frozen Lasagne
Special Tossed Green Salad
French Dressing
Fruit Compote
English Rolled Wafers (page 107)
Coffee

MENU 5

My Special Mexico Tamale Pie
Hot Tortillas
Pink Grapefruit and Avocado Salad
Relish Tray: Kumquats, Gherkins, Green Olives,
Celery Hearts, and Radishes
Lime Sherbet and Cookies
Black Coffee (lots of it too!)

MENU 6

Broiled Grapefruit
Beef Tenderloin in Pork Blanket, Baked
Baked Potatoes (page 151)
Small Ripe Tomatoes and Cucumber Sticks (page 123)
French Dressing
Hot All Bran Rolls (page 98)   Spiced Damson Plums (page 268)
Devil's Food Cake (page 102) with Caramel Icing
Iced Coffee

EMERGENCY MENUS
Menu I

Waffles (page 44)
Scrambled Eggs with Chives (page 49)
Bacon, Canadian Bacon, Chicken Livers, or Frozen Sausages
Brandied Maple Sirup   Honey   Plum Preserves
Fresh Fruit Bowl: Apples, Pears, Grapes
Coffee—More Coffee

Menu II
Baked Ham (canned)
Glazed Pineapple Slices
Yams or Sweet Potatoes (page 95)
Wedges Lettuce or Romaine with Roquefort Cheese Dressing
Hot French Bread with Garlic Butter
Vanilla Ice Cream Drenched with Rum in Parfait Glass
Pineapple Drop Cookies (page 78)

Menu III
Hot Tomato Bouillon
Tunafish Shortcake (page 239) with Mushrooms,
Pimientos, and Ripe Olives
Buttered Green Asparagus
Tray of Carrot Sticks and Cucumber Sticks (pages 93 and 123)
Home Style Canned Peach Halves with Brandy
Macaroons   Black Coffee

Menu IV
Puffed Cheese and Corn Casserole
Tossed Green Salad (page 99)
or
Ripe Red Tomatoes Sliced with
Big White Onion Circles with French Dressing
Fruit Compote (page 268) and Ginger Wafers
Hot Fragrant Tea

Menu V
My Special Clam Bowl (page 108)
or
Chilled Fruit Cocktail
Thick Slices Browned Corned Beef Hash
and
Poached Eggs
Buttered Frozen Peas
Celery or Dill Pickle Strips
Little Hot Biscuits (page 40)   Strawberry Preserves (page 265)
Coffee and More Coffee

Menu VI

Grilled Supper of
Thick Slices Ham and Potatoes
Tomatoes
Peach Halves with Currant Jelly
Whole Kernel Corn
Celery or Carrot Sticks or Finochio
Strawberry Shortcake (page 170)

How-to-do Carrot Sticks with Celery Salt

1. Scrape carrots and cut lengthwise into narrow strips.
2. Throw into a bowl of ice water and chill an hour or more.
3. Drain. Arrange crisp sticks on a tray and sprinkle generously with celery salt.
4. Bank a pile of shiny black olives across one side and there's a delightful snack bite.

HOW-TO-DO HOMEMADE VEGETABLE SOUP

A mighty good supper is homemade vegetable soup, crusty French bread, heated, dill pickles cut into strips, baked apples, and cold milk.

If you'll serve crisp hot corn pone with this just once you might be surprised. Try it instead of the French bread.

You will need:

1½ pounds lean meat and a bone with marrow
1 large can tomatoes
½ cup barley
1 large potato, diced
1 large onion, diced
3 stalks celery cut in circles (add some leaves also)
½ green pepper, cut in strips
3 carrots, sliced
Salt and pepper
½ teaspoon chili powder
1 teaspoon Worcestershire sauce
Few drops tabasco
1 tablespoon minced parsley

1. Place meat in a deep kettle and cover with cold water. Add the can of tomatoes and heat to boiling point. Add barley.

2. Turn heat down to simmer. Cover with a good tight lid and simmer until meat is nearly tender. Add more water if necessary.

3. About 30 minutes before serving, add the vegetables and seasonings and cook until done.

4. Serve in heavy deep bowls.

This soup is really better the next day as the flavors blend and ripen.

Serves 6.

How-to-do Harold's Chicken and Dumplings

1. Cook fat hen until well done, having plenty of broth in the kettle (see page 110).

2. Just before serving, drop dumplings over chicken and cook exactly 20 minutes. Do not lift the lid, not once.

3. Serve immediately.

DUMPLINGS

Sift together:

> 1¾ cups flour
> 2 teaspoons baking powder
> ½ teaspoon salt and dash red pepper

Using pastry blender, chop in 3 tablespoons shortening. Stir in ¾ cup milk to make drop dough. Drop by teaspoons into bubbling pot of stewing chicken. Cover tightly and cook 20 minutes *by the clock*. As directed above, *do not lift the lid* during this period of cooking.

Serves 4.

How-to-do Barbecued Spare Ribs

1. Buy 2 pounds spare ribs.
2. Place them in a shallow pan in HOT oven, 400 degrees, for 30 minutes.
3. Then remove ribs from oven and pour barbecue sauce over them (page 164).
4. Lower heat to moderate (325 degrees) and cook 1 hour.
5. Baste frequently with the barbecue sauce in the bottom of the roaster.
6. Cut apart with a sharp knife and serve hot.

Be sure to bring on large-sized soft paper napkins.
Chilled grapefruit sections drenched with plain French dressing is a natural with spare ribs.

Serves 4.

How-to-do Yellow Gold Yams

First, for out-of-this-world eating, bake them:

1. Select six *under* medium sized sweet potatoes, all evenly sized, not the very large ones, not the very small ones, not too big medium ones—just right ones.
2. Scrub them clean and snip off the hard ends.
3. Lay them on a wire cake rack (I don't like to put

them flat on a pan) and place in a 400-degree oven
for about 45 minutes.

4. The minute they are done remove from oven, cut
an opening on the side, and punch a chunk of butter down into the hot potato.

Eat pronto.

Now and then one will just plain burst through the
skin and all the waxy golden yam will fly over the oven.
Think nothing of it—they're worth cleaning up after and
any that is rescued is downright good. Remember how
roast pork was discovered?

New York City is a fabulous place—to coin a phrase—
but I've never grown used to being able to buy everything imaginable in this town except water-ground white
corn meal, yams, or Jonathan apples. Of course mistletoe
looks too far from home and costs more than orchids,
but it may be bought. Now if you get those strangely
tasteless colorless sweet potatoes, it really doesn't make
any particular difference *how* you cook them. However,
this is the correct way to cook yellow golden yams. Once
upon a time I heard Lowell Thomas say that he had a
standing order with a farmer in Arkansas for yams. Gives
me an idea, for they do grow to perfection in the hot
sand of Oklahoma, Louisiana, and Arkansas.

HOW-TO-DO MEXICAN TAMALE PIE

You will need:

> 8 tamales, sliced
> 1½ chicken breasts, sliced
> 1 cup grated cheese (Parmesan)

For Sauce

1 cup tomato catsup
1 cup chicken broth
½ cup chili sauce (sweet)
½ cup corn (whole-
   kernel)

1½ tablespoons olive oil
¼ cup seeded raisins, scalded
6 ripe olives cut in small
   pieces
Clove garlic

1. Simmer sauce ingredients together for 20 minutes.

2. Place in baking dish a layer of tamales, then a layer of chicken, and pour sauce on top of each layer.

3. Grate Parmesan cheese on top.

4. Bake 45 minutes in a moderate oven, 350°.

Serves 6 to 8.

HOW-TO-DO CORN BREAD SQUARES

You will need:

1 egg
2 cups buttermilk
1 teaspoon soda
1 teaspoon salt

2 cups white corn meal
   (water-ground if available)
4 tablespoons butter or bacon
   drippings

1. In a deep bowl, beat the egg till foamy and add buttermilk.

2. Stir (do not sift) soda and salt into meal and add to milk-and-egg mixture, stirring only enough to mix.

3. As you mix this have a shallow baking pan (7½ x 11 inches) with 4 tablespoons butter or bacon drippings heating in hot oven.

4. Pour hot fat into batter and quickly turn batter into sizzling hot pan. There is plenty of fat left on the pan.

5. Bake in 400-degree, hot oven for 20 minutes.

Serves 4.

Has wonderful brown shiny crust on the bottom and crisp light crust on top. Cut in squares.

HOW-TO-DO

ALL BRAN REFRIGERATOR ROLLS

These are the easiest yeast rolls I've ever made. Make them once and you'll never be afraid of yeast again.

You will need:

1 cup shortening
1 cup boiling water
½ cup sugar
1 cup All Bran
1½ teaspoons salt

2 eggs, well beaten
2 cakes compressed yeast dissolved in 1 cup lukewarm water
6 to 7 cups bread flour

1. In large bowl, mix first five ingredients listed.

2. Let stand until mixture is lukewarm in temperature.

3. Using rotary beater, beat eggs until very light and foamy.

4. Stir them into the large bowl of lukewarm ingredients. Be sure it's *lukewarm!*

5. Now stir in the yeast dissolved in the cup of *lukewarm* water.

6. Add 6 cups of flour, stirring as you add them. Beat thoroughly. If dough does not drop from spoon in definite lumps add some of that seventh cup of flour and keep adding until lumps fall from spoon (no more than 7 cups flour—not ever).

7. Brush over top of dough with melted butter and cover closely with waxed paper. Place in refrigerator for several hours, or several days.

8. *To use:* Pinch off bits of dough and form balls to fill muffin pans about half full.

9. Set in warm place to rise until double in size.*

10. Bake in hot oven, 450 degrees, for 20 minutes. Serve right out of the oven, piping hot.

Makes 3 dozen small rolls.

To make clover-leaf rolls, form 3 tiny balls, dip them in melted butter, and fit the 3 balls into 1 muffin cup. Let rise as directed and bake.

How-to-do
Tossed Green Salad with French Dressing

BOWL

1. Use wooden bowl used only for green salad and not washed.

2. Sprinkle bowl lightly with salt and then rub the surface of the bowl with a cut clove of garlic.

3. Now add crisped, well-dried, carefully torn greens. Tear greens apart with your hands. Don't cut them.

GREENS

The greens should be cleaned, crisped in the refriger-

* Place dough in warm place to rise, but not on the oven or over heat. I clear out a shelf of my cupboard, set an earthenware teapot full of boiling hot water at one end of my shelf, then place my pan of rolls at the other end of the shelf and close the door. I've tested the temperature with a thermometer and find it registers 80 degrees, and the hot water makes the air very moist, which is fine for growing plants like yeast and geraniums.

ator, and dried perfectly by patting or by blotting up all moisture. Use soft paper towels or napkins.

Small head Boston Lettuce
Bunch chicory
Bunch romaine
Bunch watercress

A few scallions or green onions, cut lengthwise into fine shreds, using some tops

FRENCH DRESSING

Into a bottle pour 6 tablespoons olive oil and 2 tablespoons wine vinegar, $\frac{1}{4}$ teaspoon salt, and plenty of freshly ground black pepper, with $\frac{1}{2}$ clove of garlic. Shake vigorously.

Add the dressing in small amounts to the prepared greens in the wooden bowl, tossing gently with a salad fork and spoon and adding dressing only as needed. Never have any amount of dressing left in the bottom of the bowl. Each leaf should be well coated with dressing, but never dripping. This is a salad delightful to eat.

HOW-TO-DO DELICIOUS CABBAGE SLAW

You will need:

1 small head cabbage
$\frac{1}{2}$ cup sour cream dressing

1. Cut a hard head of cabbage in two and remove the core, or center, at the stem end.
2. Hold the half head of cabbage, with the left hand, steady against the chopping board.
3. Cut down through the slanting cabbage head to make paper-thin slices. The knife must be razor-sharp. This method slices the cabbage into long lacy shreds. Cabbage must be chilled and crisp.

4. Pile a salad bowl nearly full and toss with sour cream dressing. (If you have a good steel slicer, use it.) Or serve in a "cabbage bowl," as suggested in my recipe for Hollowed-out Head of Cabbage (see below).

Serves 6 to 8.

Sour-cream dressing

You will need:

2 tablespoons wine vinegar	1 teaspoon celery seed
2 tablespoons sugar	½ teaspoon white mustard
½ teaspoon salt	seed
Black pepper, freshly ground	⅛ teaspoon dry mustard
1 teaspoon grated onion	½ cup sour cream

1. Heat together wine vinegar, sugar, salt, and plenty of black pepper, freshly ground, stirring gently. Let this cool.
2. Mix together grated onion, celery seed, and white mustard seed with a dash of dry mustard.
3. Stir into the sour cream and toss with the shredded cabbage, which has been well drained and dried.

Makes ½ cup dressing.

How-to-do a Cabbage Head
(Hollowed Out for a Bowl)

Buy a large head of red cabbage. It should be very hard and is more attractive if pointed in shape.

1. Cut down the natural sections, almost to the bottom of the curve (about 4 inches from the bottom end).
2. Pull the sections out gently at the top, being careful not to break the crisp cabbage.

3. Using a sharp paring knife, dig out the center to make an opening large enough to hold cabbage slaw (page 100).

4. Now turn the cabbage head upside down in a large kettle of ice-cold water and let it stay there for an hour or more. The sections will open out like petals and will curl at the tips.

5. Drain and dry carefully and place on a folded napkin on a chop plate.

6. Fill with cabbage slaw and place a serving fork and spoon beside it.

Pass to your guests and enjoy their delight.

Cabbage shell or "container" may be cut into chunks and cooked next day, so there's no waste.

HOW-TO-DO
CHOCOLATE DEVIL'S FOOD CAKE

This is one of my favorite easy cakes. I've shared it with thousands of homemakers and have heard of but one failure. That one happened because the woman insisted on adding more flour, because she said the batter seemed too thin. Don't you do that! The batter is thin, but remember that the chocolate, the egg, and the flour will all thicken as it bakes.

You will need:

1 cup sugar
¼ cup butter
¼ cup buttermilk
2 squares melted bitter chocolate

½ cup boiling water
1 egg, well beaten
1 cup all-purpose flour
¾ teaspoon baking soda
1 teaspoon baking powder

1. Just dump into a mixing bowl, without any creaming or stirring, the sugar, butter, buttermilk, and the melted chocolate.

2. Now right in on top of that add the boiling water. Stir and mix until well blended.

3. Next, stir in the egg, well beaten, and add the flour, sifted with the soda and baking powder.

4. Beat until smooth and light.

5. Pour into a 9-inch square pan or into a 7½ x 11 inch pan. I always line the bottom of my pans with a sheet of oiled waxed paper.

6. Bake in 375-degree oven for from 30 to 35 minutes.

7. Test by pressing lightly on top. When cake springs back evenly it's done. Or, a toothpick inserted in the center will come out clean when the cake is done.

8. Turn onto a wire cake cooler.

9. When cool, cover the layer with caramel icing and cut into 12 squares.

10. Or, cut the layer in two pieces and frost to make a layer cake.

EASY CARAMEL ICING

This is a fail-proof icing and is such a good taste on the devil's food cake.

You will need:

2 cups light brown sugar
½ cup cream or top milk (I sometimes use sour cream)

1 tablespoon butter
½ cup confectioners' sugar

1. Measure the sugar, milk, and butter into a saucepan.

2. Cook the brown sugar, butter, and cream together over low heat, stirring until all sugar is dissolved.

3. Then increase the heat and cook until bubbles dance all over the surface.

4. Cook for 1 minute.

5. Remove from heat and beat until slightly cooled and then add sifted confectioners' sugar.*

6. Beat until smooth and cool enough to spread.

P.S. *To my young friends:* Sometimes when Mom isn't looking it turns into mighty good candy, too. Lovingly yours, SUZIE!

How-to-do Baked Apples

Use Roman Beauty or Jonathan apples because they are firm, tart, and will stand up while baking. Use individual Pyrex dish for each apple. There is a special large size—much larger than custard cups.

1. Peel apple around top only and core.

2. Place peeled apple in dish, cover top generously with sugar, and place under broiler until nice and brown.

3. Remove from broiler, add water, and bake in oven for 45 minutes, until soft.

4. Serve, with or without cream, in dishes in which baked.

These apples are juicy, glazed on top, and delightful.

---

* It may require less confectioners' sugar at the last if cream is very thick, or if you happen to cook the mixture longer than necessary. If it should get too heavy to spread, simply place over heat a minute and beat again.

HOW-TO-DO DERA'S APPLE PIE

You will need:

A nine-inch pie pan or baking dish
6–8 Jonathan apples
1 cup sugar
1 teaspoon cinnamon
½ teaspoon nutmeg

2 teaspoons quick-cooking tapioca
2 teaspoons lemon juice
Pastry for bottom crust and lattice work for top (page 182)
2 tablespoons butter

1. Peel and cut apples into quarters or eighths, according to size.
2. Mix sugar, cinnamon, nutmeg, and tapioca together and stir through the apples. Then sprinkle with lemon juice.
3. Turn into unbaked crust. Dot on top with butter.
4. Weave lattice work covering and fit on top. Crimp edges carefully.
5. Bake in 350-degree oven for 50 minutes, then raise heat to 450 degrees to brown more quickly for about 15 minutes more.
6. Cool on wire cake rack.

HOW-TO-DO BAKED CUSTARDS

If you keep baked custards in the refrigerator you're ready for snacks, refrigerator raids, demands for a quick dessert, and many emergencies.

You will need:

3 eggs
3 tablespoons sugar
Dash salt

1 teaspoon vanilla
2½ cups milk
Nutmeg

1. Beat eggs slightly.
2. Add sugar and a dash of salt with vanilla.
3. Stir in milk.
4. Pour into lightly buttered custard cups and dust generously on top with nutmeg.
5. Set into shallow pan containing about 1 inch of water.
6. Bake in a 350-degree oven for 25 to 35 minutes, or until a silver knife comes out clean when placed in the center of the custard.

Serves 4 to 6.

HOW-TO-DO MAYE'S GINGERBREAD

You will need:

½ cup sugar	1½ cups flour (all-purpose)
½ cup shortening	2 teaspoons each of nutmeg,
½ cup sorghum	cinnamon, allspice, and
1 egg	ginger
½ cup hot water	1 teaspoon soda

1 cup raisins

1. Mix sugar, shortening, sorghum, and egg yolk, and beat well.
2. Add hot water and beat quickly.
3. Sift flour (save out a little), spices, and soda and add to mixture, beating well.
4. Dredge raisins in remaining flour and stir them through the batter.
5. Beat egg white until stiff and fold it through batter.
6. Pour into 7½ x 11 inch pan, well greased.

7. Bake in 350-degree oven 45 minutes.
8. Serve hot.

   Serves 6.

How-to-do English Rolled Wafers

These are festive crisp cookies and after you do the first panful you'll suddenly decide they are as easy as can be. I did them for a garden party one time and made 390 of them. The rolling stunt was automatic by the time I finished. And I also had discovered all the easy tricks.

1. In a heavy saucepan, heat ½ cup molasses to the boiling point.
2. Stir in ½ cup butter or margarine.
3. Add 1 cup flour sifted with 2/3 cup sugar and 1 tablespoon ginger. Add dry ingredients slowly, stirring constantly. Beat well.
4. Drop by small spoonfuls onto well-oiled cooky sheet, leaving fully 2 inches between cookies, as they spread a lot while baking.
5. Place in 300-degree oven to bake about 15 minutes.
6. Remove from oven and carefully loosen wafers around the edge. Now quickly roll wafer over the handle of a wooden spoon. They look like rolled pancakes, only of course they're crisp and lacy.

When I made 390 I learned:

   a. Don't let wafers cool in a draft. Try to roll them while hot. If they get cool they will harden and not roll.
   b. Always let cooky sheet cool before dropping second

batch on, because wafers will spread less on cool sheet.

c. Use a small spoon and dip a level amount, never heaped. Actually a level ½ teaspoon is enough.

d. If wafers harden before they are all rolled, they should be set back in a warm oven a minute and then rolled quickly.

e. They should be kept in a tightly covered tin box.

Sometimes I add ½ cup finely ground pecans to the batter.

You'll get 3 dozen wafers from this amount and they are delicious.

DINNER SOUPS

HOW-TO-DO MINCED CLAM SOUP

You will need:

7-ounce can minced clams (Pioneer brand)	1 stalk celery with leaves
	1 slice onion
2 cups top milk	Freshly ground black pepper
1 tablespoon butter	Salt

2 butter crackers

1. Pour minced clams into heavy saucepan.

2. Add top milk (half cream—if it's the day), butter, celery with leaves, onion, plenty of freshly ground black pepper, and only a small dash of salt.

3. Simmer over LOW heat, stirring for about 10 minutes. DO NOT BOIL.

4. *To serve:* Heat bowls really hot. Keep soup HOT. Remove celery and onion and throw away. Crumble 2

butter crackers in the hot soup and quickly pour soup into hot bowls.

Serves 4.

This is just a poem of a soup, but I warn you it *must* be hot. Also, I've never found anything but Pioneer brand which made it perfectly.

HOW-TO-DO OYSTER STEW

You must be gentle in handling each step of the creation of an oyster stew. Just heat the rich milk, don't boil it. Barely heat the fresh oysters, till plump, not curled and hard. Lightly season it all to point up, but not overshadow, the true flavor of fresh oysters. Keep heat *low*.

1 pint fresh oysters in their own liquor	Chunk of butter (at least 1 tablespoon)
1 quart milk (or half milk and half cream)	½ teaspoon salt and ½ teaspoon paprika
Freshly ground black pepper	

1. Heat the oyster liquor with the butter and all the seasonings, *simmering* together about 4 minutes.
2. Scald the milk.
3. Now add the oysters and simmer gently over LOW heat, watching carefully. Don't wait for them to curl on the edges even.
4. Just the second they are plumped out and hot all the way through, add the scalded milk and stir together to blend the flavors.
5. Keep over *low, low* heat, or better still over hot water, till served.

6. Turn into heated bowls and eat with rapt attention and appreciation.

Serves 4.

HOW-TO-DO MEAT STOCK

Every good manager at home should keep a jar of stock in her refrigerator. This is the liquid to be added to braised meats and once you use it you never will use just plain water. Use it also in soups, sauces, etc.

Stock should be cooled quickly. Fat will rise to the top and become solid. This acts as a seal, which should not be broken until ready to use stock. Keep in coldest part of refrigerator. If not used in a couple of days, reheat to boiling and cool again quickly.

You will need:

4 pounds meat and bone (ask market man to crack bones)
3 quarts cold water
2 tablespoons fat
½ teaspoon salt
4 cloves, 1 bay leaf

5 peppercorns
1 large onion
2 carrots
2 or 3 sprigs parsley
1 or 2 stalks celery, including leaves

1. Cut meat in small cubes.
2. Put 2/3 of meat cubes into heavy kettle. Add bones, seasonings, and water.
3. In heavy skillet, heat 2 tablespoons fat and brown meat cubes.
4. Add these to soup kettle and bring it to a boil. Put good tight lid on and simmer 3 hours.
5 Add vegetables and simmer one hour more.
6. Strain.

Makes 2¼ quarts rich stock.

MEATS

Next to your husband, your meatman should be your best friend. Cultivate him.

Shop in slack hours, if possible. Ask him to show you cuts of meat. Learn what, where, why. Buy with his help and let him know you are following his advice. This pays real dividends.

I urge you to learn TWO definitions today and make them your own:

ONE: *There are only two methods of meat cookery.* They are by DRY, DIRECT HEAT and by MOIST HEAT.

TWO: ROASTING AND BROILING are done by the dry, direct heat method. BRAISING is cooking by long, slow, moist heat.

The ways of cooking *all the meats* you see in your markets divide themselves into these two methods.

The more tender (and more expensive) cuts of meat have little exercise, so the connective tissue is tender and dissolves under direct, dry heat. We pay more for them and use less time cooking them, by roasting or broiling.

The less tender (and less expensive) cuts of meat have more exercise, so the connective tissue is less tender and they require long, slow, moist cookery to dissolve these tissues and make the meat juicy and tender. So we pay less for these cuts of meat and spend more time cooking them. But note: the nourishment is the same in one pound of actual lean porterhouse (expensive) and one pound of actual lean shoulder or shank (less expensive) meat.

Meat Cuts and How to Cook Them
BEEF CHART

Retail Cuts — Wholesale Cuts — Retail Cuts

Ground Beef — Heel of Round
— Roast or Broil — Braise or Simmer —

Hind Shank
— Soup or Simmer —

Rolled Flank — Flank Stew
— Braise — — Stew —

Flank Steak — Flank Steak Fillets
— Braise —

Plate Boiling Beef — Rolled Plate — Short Ribs
— Simmer or Braise —

Beef Brisket — Corned Beef
— Simmer —

Knuckle Soup Bone — Cross Cut Fore Shank
— Soup or Braise —

English Cut — Arm Pot Roast — Arm Steak
— Braise —

ROUND — RUMP — LOIN END — FLANK — SHORT LOIN — PLATE — RIB — BRISKET — SHANK — CHUCK

Round Steak — Top Round — Bottom Round (Swiss Steak)
— Braise —

Rolled Rump — Rump Roast
— Braise or Roast —

Sirloin Steak — Pin Bone Sirloin Steak
— Broil or Panbroil —

Porterhouse Steak — T Bone Steak — Club Steak
— Broil or Panbroil —

Standing Rib Roast — Rolled Rib Roast — Rib Steak
— Roast — — Broil —

Blade Steak — Blade Pot Roast

Triangle Pot-Roast — Boneless Chuck Pot-Roast — Shoulder Fillet
— Braise —

Rolled Neck — Boneless Neck
— Braise or Stew —

How-to-buy and How-to-cook Meat

Buy a whole ham and ask your meat-market man to cut it for you so that you don't "ham the family" to weariness. You'll find a complete HOW-TO-DO method and recipes for this on page 124.

Sometimes buy a leg of lamb and follow the same steps. See HOW-TO-DO's on page 120.

Remember, there are only TWO ways to cook meat:

    (1) By dry direct heat.
    (2) By moist heat.

     (1) Dry heat is broiling or roasting.
     (2) Moist heat is braising or stewing or boiling.

So as you look at the meat in the market counter, remember it is all to be cooked by one or the other of these two methods.

How-to-do Roast Beef Standing Ribs

("Roasting is dry direct heat")

1. Place the ribs, fat side up, in a shallow roasting pan. The bones serve as a rack, keeping the meat off of the pan.
2. Place the meat in a 350-degree oven. DO NOT COVER. DO NOT ADD ANY WATER OR OTHER LIQUID. Roasting is *dry direct* heat!
3. Roast in this 350-degree oven, allowing 19 minutes to the pound for rare meat; 22 minutes to the pound for medium; and 25 minutes per pound for well-done meat.
4. No basting is necessary, as the fat drips over the meat and it is basted thoroughly.
5. Add salt and pepper and serve from a heated platter—

immediately. Cut across the grain of the meat and carve thin slices.

A two-rib roast (7 to 8 pounds) serves 8 to 10.

Rib roast is a temperamental star and should be served as soon as it's done, for it is at its peak of perfection the minute it's taken out of the oven.

How-to-do Natural Beef Gravy or Sauce

1. Remove roast to heated platter. Work quickly.
2. Pour off excess fat.
3. Place roasting pan over high heat on top burner of range and scrape off all brown particles, stirring them into the fat and juices.
4. Now quickly dash ¼ cup water into the roaster and stir well. Taste for seasonings.
5. Pour into very hot bowl.

Nice to serve a bit of this with each slice of roast.

HOW-TO-DO CONSERVATION BEEF

Buy a large cut of beef rump, from 5 to 7 pounds. This is superior meat and there will be no leftover worries, I assure you.

For this you will also need:

½ pound smoked ham from hock end
Marinade of ¼ cup wine vinegar and ¼ cup olive oil
1 clove garlic

½ cup hot tomato juice
½ cup hot stock
2 stalks celery with leaves
A few slices of carrot
1 onion

1. Remove practically all fat from beef.
2. Cut lean strips of ham about ½ inch thick and about 2 inches long.

3. Using a sharp, short paring knife, gash holes in the roast, and force these strips of ham into the openings.

4. Let the end of the ham strip protrude just a bit, so that when you have finished the meat will have a burry appearance.

5. Now place it in a deep bowl and drip the marinade over, turning frequently.

6. Let stand at least an hour, or longer. Insert 1 clove garlic. If you have time leave overnight in refrigerator to stay in marinade. Turn in marinade several times.

7. Rub surface of heavy roaster with suet and sear meat on all sides until deep brown and crusty.

8. Add the hot rich stock and hot tomato juice with 2 stalks of celery (including leaves), a few slices of carrot, and an onion.

9. Cover with tight lid. Braise in low moderate oven, 325 degrees, allowing 35 minutes to the pound.

10. Let stand in the rich liquor, turning once or twice, until time to serve. Keep hot.

Serves 10 to 12.

For sandwich material, dip slices of meat back into the savory juice before fitting them between rye-bread slices. Add a paper-thin slice of onion, too. Or try horse-radish spread for a change.

How To Pan-broil a T-bone Steak or Lamb Chops

1. Heat heavy skillet sizzling hot.

2. Rub a small bit of the fat from the meat over surface of hot skillet.

3. Keep heat high.

4. Place steak or chops in skillet. Be careful that chops do not touch each other. Also be sure to press meat lightly against the hot skillet to form a tight seal. Don't move until ready to turn.

5. As soon as meat has had time to brown turn heat down a little to medium high.

6. The minute any fat accumulates in skillet, pour it off. Hold meat in place with turner or with a lid. Keep *all* fat poured off. We are broiling, not frying.

7. Turn when well browned and broil other side.

8. Don't overcook. Meat should be pink, juicy, and tender. Until you learn to judge accurately, cut a slight gash into meat to see when it suits you.

9. When done place on heated platter and serve immediately. This kind of meat doesn't wait.

NOTE: To broil on broiler rack, simply place meat on rack in preheated broiler. Meat should be about 2½ inches below flame or unit. Keep heat high. Turn and cook to suit taste.

HOW-TO-DO BEEF OR LAMB STEW

You will need:

2 pounds beef or lamb, chuck or even neck meat, cut in large cubes	A few drops of tabasco sauce
	2 cups stock or tomato juice
¼ cup flour	4 stalks celery
4 tablespoons fat	6 small carrots
1 teaspoon soy sauce	2 medium-sized potatoes
1 teaspoon chili powder	1 large onion
1 bay leaf	1 cup green peas
	2 teaspoons salt

¼ teaspoon black pepper

1. Roll meat in flour until well coated.
2. In heavy skillet with a good tight lid, heat fat sizzling hot.
3. *Brown* meat cubes quickly.
4. Add 1 teaspoon soy sauce, 1 teaspoon chili powder, 1 bay leaf, a few drops of tabasco sauce, and the stock or juice.
5. Cover with a *good tight lid* and *simmer* for 1 hour.
6. If necessary, add 1 cup more of stock or juice and then place vegetables cut into large chunks over the stew. Sprinkle generously with salt and pepper.
7. Cover and simmer for about 45 minutes, or until vegetables are tender.

Serves 6 to 8.

The stew should be moist and soupy, but not too thin. The less tender meat will require longer cooking. When finished, you should be able to cut the meat with a fork and it should be rich, brown, and savory, with a rich, smooth gravy sauce.

How-to-do Sautéed Calf's Liver—Different

I've seen "liver haters" eat liver prepared by this method and declare it the best they'd ever eaten and that it was the first time they ever really liked liver.

1. Ask your market man to slice the liver paper-thin. This is the No. 1 *must*. If not thinly sliced, too much cooking time is required and the liver becomes toughened and dry.

2. Pour V-8 Cocktail juice into a shallow dish and add 1 cut clove of garlic.

3. Place the slices of liver in this juice, being sure each slice is well covered with the juice.

4. Turn the slices frequently and let them stand in this juice for from 15 minutes to a half hour, or longer.

5. Using a fork, hold each slice up to drain well, then dip it into a mound of flour to which salt and pepper have been added.

6. When each side is coated with flour, sauté the portions in a small amount of butter, or use bacon or ham drippings, if you prefer.

7. Keep heat moderate and amount of fat just enough to cover the bottom of the skillet. Never swim the liver in fat. Sauté just 1½ minutes to each side.

8. Remove heated platter and garnish with crisply broiled bacon strips and sprigs of fresh parsley.

9. Serve immediately. Liver is so tender and moist it may easily be cut with a fork.

One pound serves 3 to 4.

How-to-do Plain Hamburgers

For the very best Hamburgers, buy chuck from the best beef. Of course, steer is tops for this buy. Ground round is dry and less flavorful. The ground meat found in most counter displays is not nearly as good a buy as the chuck. Try it just one time and see how much better your Hamburgers are. It will cost more than counter meat, but I assure you that you'll get much more for your money.

From one pound chuck, you will be able to make five medium-thick patties. For plain Hamburgers, do not add any seasonings. Handle the meat *very gently,* patting it lightly into shape. Do NOT press or smash to flatten the meat, even if you like them thin, for it is just as easy to form Hamburgers lightly and keep them moist and fluffy.

TO BROIL

1. Place on oiled broiler rack just under the heat and broil for 1½ minutes to each side for thick rare, for 2 minutes to each side for medium.
2. Add salt and pepper and serve immediately, or sooner!

TO PAN-BROIL

1. Lightly *coat* a heavy skillet with butter and when the skillet is very hot, pan-broil Hamburgers, turning one time.
2. Press the edges close to the skillet, but do not flatten the meat or press on center of patties.
3. Add salt and freshly ground black pepper just as you lift them to toasted buttered buns.

Sometimes brush the buns on the top crust with beaten egg and sprinkle with sesame seed, then heat buns in the oven to set the seeds. Split, butter, and toast for Hamburgers. Mighty good variation, says Susan!

One pound Hamburger makes 4 big patties.

How-to-do London Broil

Nice only if perfectly timed.

Ask your market man to cut these slices for you. He's an expert and this flank steak *must* be cut on the bias and paper-thin. Broil the slices just long enough to heat through—not even one minute. Serve immediately, or even sooner!

London broil is usually served with a broiled kidney and a sausage. One of each to a serving.

How-to-do Leg o' Lamb

1. Buy a leg of lamb weighing about 7 pounds. To use this amount of meat wisely and not to "lamb your family to boredom," first cut off the shank end, cutting up nice big chunks to be turned into stew.
2. Wrap this and place it in the coldest (not freezing) section of your refrigerator for use later.
3. Next, cut three chops from the other end, the larger end, of the lamb and pan-broil them for dinner. Now you have about a 4-pound leg-of-lamb roast left.

Leg of lamb managed this way will supply half a dozen completely different menus—not akin to the usual leftovers.

How-to-do Lamb Roast

1. Place lamb, fat side up, on a rack in a shallow roasting pan.
2. Set in 325-degree oven to roast for about 2 hours. Do NOT COVER. DO NOT ADD WATER OR ANY OTHER LIQUID.
3. Allow 30 minutes per pound for this 4-pound roast. For the whole leg-of-lamb roast, allow 20 minutes per pound—this means of course when you do not cut any of it off, for chops or for stew.

4. Add salt and pepper and place on sizzling hot platter to serve piping hot.

Carve *across the grain* in thin slices. Serve lamb very hot, or serve it icy cold.

How-to-do Pan-broiled Lamb Chops

DEFINITION: Broiling is cooking by *dry, direct heat!* Now for pan-broiled lamb chops:

1. Buy loin lamb chops 1½ inches thick.
2. Trim off part of the fat around the edges.
3. Fasten long end of meat around chop, using a toothpick to hold it.
4. Turn heat high to heat heavy ungreased skillet.
5. When skillet is piping hot, hold a chop in your hand and rub the fat portion quickly over the surface of the hot skillet, just to form a coating.
6. Now place the chops in the very hot skillet, pressing them onto it to form a perfect seal.
7. Do not let chops touch each other as they will create steam.
8. The minute any fat accumulates in the pan, quickly pour it off.
9. When about half done, turn and finish broiling.
10. KEEP ALL FAT POURED OFF, or the chops will be *fried,* not broiled.
11. Lamb is best cooked medium and chops 1½ inches thick require about 10 to 12 minutes. When done, add salt and pepper and serve immediately from heated platter.

HOW TO VARY LAMB CHOPS

Place chops on a hot platter, then scrape all crustiness from the pan, add 2 teaspoons butter, and a dash of salt and pepper. When very, very hot, dash in about 4 tablespoons white wine, a little at a time. Let it bubble and steam up and then pour it over the chops. Perfect!

HOW-TO-COOK A TONGUE

You will need:

4 pounds smoked tongue	Thick slice of onion
1 stalk celery with leaves	1 cup applesauce
1 tablespoon prepared horse-radish	

1. Place tongue in a large kettle with hot water to cover the tongue well.
2. Add 1 stalk and leaves of celery, a thick slice of onion, and several peppercorns.
3. Put a good tight lid on after this comes to a boil.
4. Turn the heat down to a low simmer and keep it that way for $3\frac{1}{2}$ hours, or until the tongue is so tender it is easily pierced with a fork. The small bones at the base of the tongue will slip out easily when the tongue is done.
5. Let it cool in the liquor.
6. Lift the tongue out onto a piece of waxed paper and slit the tough skin with a sharp knife.
7. Holding the tip of the tongue toward you, rounded side up, pull the skin away. It slips off just like a glove.
8. Now cut the bony, gristly portion off, and the very tip end.

(Use these pieces to grind up for sandwiches. Mix with mustard or horse-radish and they're nice on rye bread. Keep in refrigerator for emergencies too.)

9. You are ready to slice the tongue into very thin slices now and it should be carved on the bias.

10. Arrange on a hot plate and serve with applesauce mixed with horse-radish.

Serves 6 to 8.

NOTE: Pass a tray of crisp cucumber sticks. Do NOT feel that spinach must be urged on this day. That's why many folks think they do not like tongue. Instead, serve crisp watercress salad, cucumber sticks, and special applesauce.

Special Applesauce

Mix 2 tablespoons horse-radish and 2 teaspoons lemon juice into 2 cups chilled applesauce.

Cucumber Sticks

Peel a cucumber. Cut it into lengthwise strips. Chill it thoroughly. Sprinkle with lime juice *when ready to serve.*

How-to-do Baked Ham

1. Score (cut) the fat portion, making large squares or diamonds.
2. Place two or three cloves in the center of each square.
3. Brush with mustard.
4. Pat about 1 cup brown sugar onto the surface.
5. Place the ham on a rack in an open roaster.
6. Pour 1 cup pickled peach juice around the meat.

7. Bake in a 350-degree oven, basting now and then with the juice.

From ¼ to ½ pound of meat is allowed for a serving. Whole hams vary in size.

Processed or Precooked: Allow 10 minutes per pound.

Unprocessed Ham: Allow 25 to 30 minutes per pound.

How to Plan for a Whole Ham

Here's how to manage a whole ham, which is the economical way to buy ham, and still not *ham* the family to boredom before it is gone.

1. Buy an 11-pound ham. Ask your market man to cut it in two, leaving the butt end whole. It will weigh about 6 pounds. This leaves about 5 pounds in the shank end.

2. Then ask him to cut a thick center cut off the butt end. Wrap this slice in waxed paper and put it into the refrigerator to broil for dinner next week some time.

3. Prepare the butt end to bake for Sunday dinner (see page 123).

4. Also ask your market man to cut the shank in two, lengthwise, leaving all the bone on one side.

5. From the bone portion cut out chunks of ham sufficient to grind for ham patties. Make this into patties, wrap them around with strips of bacon, and place them in waxed paper to store in refrigerator for breakfast, any day next week.

6. The bone portion is mighty good to cook with beans, with other vegetables, or for split-pea soup.

7. The heavy portion of the shank is cut away to be used for slices to fry. The end portion is ground for ham loaf, or it may be cut into chunks to be used in casserole dishes.

The ham will keep when managed this way and may be used as the family really wants it.

HOW-TO-DO SUSAN'S VEAL CHOPS

Grand company meat . . . looks important . . . never forgotten.

You will need:

4 loin veal chops	¾ cup red wine
1 egg	6 black olives, slivered
2 tablespoons cold water	1 teaspoon minced parsley
Fine dry crumbs	Pinch sweet marjoram
2 tablespoons butter	Spiced crab apples (optional)

1. Dip loin veal chops in flour, to which salt and pepper have been added.
2. In a shallow bowl, mix egg with cold water.
3. Dip chops into egg mixture, coating each side.
4. Then dip them into a mound of powdered dry bread crumbs.
5. Heat butter in a heavy skillet and brown the chops carefully.
6. When well browned, add red wine, the black olives, slivered, minced parsley, and a pinch of sweet marjoram.
7. Cover with tight lid and simmer over *low* heat for from thirty to forty minutes. The chops should be so tender they may be cut with a fork.

8. Place on a heated platter and pour sauce over them. Garnish with spiced crab apples.

HOW-TO-DO PARISIAN VEAL

This recipe I got in a little, but wonderful restaurant in Paris.

You will need:

1 pound special veal steaks	2 tablespoons cold water
1 egg	Powdered bread crumbs
	2 tablespoons butter

Have portions cut from veal steaks at the "seams." These are portions smaller than the palm of my hand. They are cut *with* the grain of the meat, from the leg of veal. Ask your market man to split them with a sharp knife so each piece will open out flat. Then have him cover them with parchment paper and smash them with a mallet. They'll be paper-thin.

1. Dip veal slices into mixture of 1 egg beaten with 2 tablespoons cold water.

2. Then into a mound of powdered bread crumbs.

3. Sauté in butter just until browned and crisply tender —only a few minutes.

4. Remove to hot platter and place a very thin slice of lime on each piece. Top the lime slice with a tiny butter ball into which minced parsley is rolled.

Be sure to have butter balls all made, lime sliced paper-thin, platter very hot, and guests or family seated at table before veal is ready to take up to serve. It's no good if it has to wait at all. But be assured it's worth waiting for.

Serves 4.

I always serve green peas in lettuce leaves (page 157), thinly sliced tomatoes, new radishes, scalloped potatoes, toasted French rolls, and fresh strawberries with this delicate veal serving.

HOW-TO-DO VEAL CASSEROLE

"Give us one-piece dinners" is the request from new homemakers as well as from old timers. After all, this is a streamlined age and menus have long needed simplifying. When meat, vegetables, and delicious gravy, with a topping of biscuits or dumplings, is prepared for dinner, there's little more required.

You will need:

2 pounds veal shoulder or veal breast	6 carrots
⅓ pound salt pork	4 small onions
2 cups hot stock	1 cup diced celery
	Salt, pepper, thyme

Drop biscuits (page 169)

1. Cut salt pork into cubes and brown quickly in heavy skillet. Take up as soon as brown and keep in dish.

2. Cut veal into generous cubes and roll in flour until well coated.

3. Now brown the veal quickly in the hot salt-pork fat, turning frequently. Add salt, pepper, and thyme.

4. As soon as veal is browned, add the salt pork and 2 cups hot stock (see page 110), or if not veal stock, add chicken-bouillon cube dissolved in hot water.

5. Cover with that good tight lid and simmer over low heat for about 1½ hours, or until meat is so tender it may be cut with a fork.

6. About 20 minutes before meat is done, add small whole onions and the carrots cut into good-sized chunks, also the celery, cut in thick circles.

7. Cook again at simmering heat until vegetables are tender but not overcooked. Gravy should be rich and thick.

8. Pour all this stew into a casserole and top with pinwheel or with drop biscuits and bake in hot oven, 425 degrees, for 20 minutes.

Serves 4 to 6.

The stew may be made early in the day and topped with biscuits just before serving. If the gravy seems a bit thin when the vegetables are added, just grate a medium-sized potato into the stew, which will thicken it nicely and add flavor also.

Serve with thick slices tomato and crisp cucumber sticks sprinkled generously with lime juice.

Big juicy baked apples, oatmeal cookies, and hot tea complete an economical as well as delicious dinner.

HOW-TO-DO STUFFED PORK CHOPS BRAISED
(For Two)

Buy 2 shoulder chops. Have a pocket cut in each one. This pocket should extend clear across the chops.

1. Prepare and pour into a bowl the following ingredients:

1 cup dry bread crumbs
1 stalk celery, finely minced
1 medium-sized onion, diced
and sautéed in butter
Cider or apple juice
1 tablespoon minced parsley
½ teaspoon salt and plenty of
black pepper
1 unpeeled apple, chopped

2. Mix all ingredients except cider or apple juice.

3. Stir in cider or apple juice until the mixture is moist and holds together, but is not pasty.

4. Stuff this dressing into the pockets and fasten with toothpicks.

5. Dust the chops with flour to which salt and pepper have been added.

6. Brown the chops in a heavy skillet, using only enough fat to prevent burning.

7. Turn and brown on other side.

8. Add 1 cup warm (don't boil) cider, or apple juice.

9. Put on a good tight lid and bake in a 325-degree oven for 1½ hours.

10. Remove the lid during the last fifteen minutes of cooking, to brown and crisp on top.

11. Serve with chilled applesauce. I sometimes like to add 1 tablespoon horse-radish to 1 cup applesauce to go with pork. Garnish with watercress.

HOW-TO-DO STUFFED PORK CHOP ROAST
(For a Small Family)

1. Buy 3 thick loin pork chops.

2. Using the same stuffing given for braised chops (page 128), pat a generous portion of it over the first chop and then stack the second chop on top.

3. Next, cover that chop with all the stuffing it will hold and top with the third chop.

4. Fasten with skewers and tie securely with soft cord.

5. Place in shallow pan, bone side down, fat side up. No water. No lid.

6. Roast, uncovered, at 350 degrees for about 2 hours, or 35 minutes per pound.
   Serves 3 generously.

HOW-TO-DO VEAL CURRY

Every homemaker is interested in making a little meat go a long way. With 1½ pounds of veal from a less expensive cut four can be served generously. Here is a simple curry adaptation. The spiced peach conserve is a substitute for chutney. It's an old favorite of ours.

You will need:

1½ pounds veal
4 tablespoons flour
2 tablespoons best-grade curry powder
¼ teaspoon salt
¼ teaspoon pepper
1 egg
4 tablespoons butter or chicken fat
1 cup hot consommé or stock

1. Sift flour, curry powder, salt, and pepper together.

2. Cut veal in serving portions.

3. Dip each piece in the beaten egg, then in the flour mixture. Let stand a minute, then repeat, dipping again in egg, then in crumbs.

4. In heavy skillet, heat 4 tablespoons butter or chicken fat. Brown veal on both sides.

5. Add 1 cup hot consommé or stock.

6. Cover and cook slowly in low moderate oven, 325 degrees, for 40 minutes.

7. Uncover and add spiced peach conserve. Cook another 10 minutes. Serve on bed of fluffy white rice on heated platter.

Serves 4 to 6.

Spiced Peach Conserve

Combine 1 cup canned peaches and juice with 1 cup sugar, 2 tablespoons seeded raisins (plumped), ½ dozen whole cloves, 2 tablespoons lemon juice. Let sugar dissolve over low heat, then simmer gently for 20 minutes. Remove cloves.

POULTRY

How-to-do Fried Chicken

Fried chicken must be golden brown, with a crisp juicy skin, not hard or dry. The meat must be moist and tender and white all the way to the bone—none of that awful pinkish color around the bone.

1. Wash chicken thoroughly under cold-water faucet. Don't ever soak in water.

2. Pat perfectly dry with soft paper toweling.

3. Add salt and black pepper to ½ cup flour and pour it into a paper sack.

4. Drop the pieces of chicken into the sack and shake hard until each piece is lightly coated.

5. In heavy skillet, having tight seal lid, heat fat. I use ¼ cup shortening and ¼ cup butter. It should be very hot, but never let the butter scorch.

6. Shake surplus flour from chicken and arrange chicken in hot fat in skillet.

7. Place heavy pieces, thighs and breasts, in the center of the skillet, fitting bony pieces around the edge.

8. Keep heat medium high and brown evenly, but not too fast. Remember, the skin must be crisp and lacy —not hard.

9. Turn and brown other side.

10. Now turn the heat down just as low as it will go and put the good tight lid on.

11. Let cook for from 45 minutes to 1 hour, depending on size of fryer. Shift pieces around in pan and turn as necessary. Keep tightly covered until done.

12. Taste for salt and add plenty of freshly ground black pepper while cooking.

13. Remove to heated platter and make cream gravy (see below).

Serves 4 approximately.

HOW-TO-DO CHICKEN CREAM GRAVY

1. In the skillet, over low-moderate heat, leave 6 tablespoons of chicken fat.

2. With a wooden spoon, scrape all crusty pieces from the skillet.

3. Stir in 3 level tablespoons flour and stir flour and fat together until perfectly smooth and very lightly browned. Keep heat moderate.

4. Now add 3 cups cold milk and stir rapidly over high heat.

5. Cook until smooth and slightly thickened.

6. Add salt and black pepper and pour into *very* hot gravy boat. Serve over hot biscuits, and enjoy yourself.

HOW-TO-DO BARBECUED CHICKEN

You will need:

1 large fryer
1 cup olive oil
1 clove garlic
1 cup barbecue sauce (page 164)

1. Cut the fryer into pieces and wipe them perfectly dry.

2. Arrange pieces in a shallow dish or platter.

3. Pour the olive oil over the chicken and drop in the clove of garlic.

4. Turn the pieces of chicken over occasionally. Let stand in the refrigerator several hours, or overnight.

5. Remove pieces and drain slightly.

6. Place in heavy aluminum or iron skillet and brown over medium heat uncovered. Use only enough oil in the bottom of the skillet to prevent burning, as the chicken is so drenched in oil.

7. Turn and when browned on both sides add the heated barbecue sauce, pouring it all over the chicken.

8. Put on a good tight lid and place in 325-degree oven to cook slowly for from 1 to 1½ hours, depending on the size of the fryer.

This must cook until the meat literally does drop from the bones. Check it toward the latter part of the cooking time. It must not cook too fast or cook dry. If it should get too dry, or if reheated the next day, add red wine which has been heated and cover to cook gently till moist and hot all the way through.

Serve on a heated platter garnished with pickled peaches. Buttered rice is mighty correct with this, too.

Serves 4 approximately.

HOW-TO-DO

CHICKEN PIE WITH PIN-WHEEL BISCUITS

This dish, with a salad, and fruit for dessert, makes a whole meal. Easy and economical and always a favorite. Note that some of the ingredients are listed with the mixing directions. Buy bony pieces of chicken.

You will need:

2 cups chicken	1 cup peas
½ cup celery	2 cups chicken stock

1. Cover chicken with 2½ cups water. Add celery leaves, a thick slice of onion, and a few peppercorns for seasoning.
2. Bring to a boil and then cut heat to a low simmer.
3. Cover with tight lid and cook until meat falls from bones.
4. Let cool in liquor.
5. Remove chicken from bone. Cut skin very fine. Add frozen or fresh peas and tender celery cut into good bite-sized pieces.
6. Turn all into a casserole.
7. Strain stock and thicken by adding: 1 tablespoon flour mixed to a smooth paste with 2 or 3 tablespoons stock,

then stirred into the 2 cups of stock as it cooks about 10 minutes.

8. Now add 2 beaten egg yolks, first stirring a little of the hot stock into the yolks to prevent curdling. Cook gently for 2 minutes. Now you have a perfect rich chicken sauce to pour over the ingredients in the casserole.

9. Top with pin-wheel biscuits and bake in a hot oven (400 degrees) for 25 minutes.

Serves 4 to 6.

How-to-make Pin-wheel Biscuits

Use biscuit mix, chopping in 1/3 cup more shortening to 2 cups. Then follow recipe on package for biscuits. Roll very thin to form rectangle and sprinkle with 2 minced pimientos and ½ shredded green pepper. Then roll up as for a jelly roll and cut into ½-inch slices. Pull apart slightly and place atop casserole.

HOW-TO-DO
FLORENCE AND BILL'S CHICKEN LOAF

You will need:

1 fat hen simmered well done, cooled in its broth and chopped	¾ quart milk
	2 cups soft bread crumbs
1 cup cooked rice	1 tablespoon salt
3 eggs, well beaten	¼ cup chicken fat
	1 tablespoon paprika

1. Combine ingredients in order listed.
2. Pour into buttered loaf pan.

3. Bake one hour in 350-degree oven.
4. Let stand 15 minutes before cutting.
   Serves 8.

Gravy

Make gravy by adding 2 tablespoons flour to a little cold chicken stock and stirring to make a smooth paste. Next, stir this paste into 2 cups of chicken stock and cook until slightly thickened and smooth. Add:

1 cup cooked chopped celery	½ can pimientos
1 can drained mushrooms	1 cup milk

HOW-TO-DO TURKEY OR CHICKEN STOCK

Please do make this good stock for your turkey stuffing and for gravy. It is so much better than water!

You will need:

All the neck, the gizzard, the heart, and the *feet* (ask for them).

BOUQUET

2 stalks celery with leaves	1 teaspoon salt
1 medium onion	1 bay leaf
1 carrot	A few peppercorns
5 cups cold water	

1. Pour water over chicken pieces and bouquet.
2. Bring to boiling point.
3. Reduce heat to simmer. Put good tight lid on and simmer 1 to 4 hours, the longer the better.
4. Lift out bones, skin, and seasoning bouquet. Be sure to remove peppercorns. You may strain through a coarse sieve if you prefer.

How-to-do Roast Turkey

I'm always thankful for letters received from my young homemakers at Thanksgiving time. "Well, my mother-in-law said mine was the best turkey and stuffing she ever ate. I followed your directions step by step and it really was perfect. Gee I was proud and it didn't seem hard to do after all."

This is quoted for your encouragement.

1. Be sure your turkey is perfectly cleaned and ready the *morning* before. Remove all pinfeathers, wash thoroughly inside, and remove all spongy portions along ribs and backbone, rinsing in cold water.

2. Using soft paper toweling pat *dry* inside and outside. Rub lightly inside with salt. Wrap in waxed paper and place in refrigerator.

3. Now make the turkey stuffing. This takes time, but may be wedged in between other chores (see page 138).

4. Use a very large pan to mix stuffing in and be sure to give it time to stand until perfectly cold. Important.

5. Now stuff and truss your turkey the last thing at night. Fill the cavity, but do not pack it too full. Stuffing will expand as it bakes.

6. Fasten opening together with light metal skewers, then lace skewers together with soft cord.

7. Turn the bird over and fill neck opening. Fasten neck skin tightly against backbone, using long, heavy skewer.

8. Turn bird on its back and run 2 long skewers

through the legs, fastening them down close to the tail.

9. Take a long piece of soft cord and hold the ends even. Catch the middle of the cord around the wings and cross it over to come down the back so you can easily loop each cord over ends of leg skewers. Tie legs close to tail and the turkey is trussed.

10. Keep in refrigerator where there is plenty of air circulation around it. Don't pile food around it.

11. *To Roast:* Place on rack. Rub breast and joints *lightly* with turkey paste (page 140). Set in oven, 325 degrees, to roast. Allow 20 minutes to the pound for a 12-pound turkey and about 15 minutes to the pound for a 20-pound turkey and 25 minutes per pound for a small turkey, 8 pounds, say. If you have a turkey over 18 pounds set oven at 300 degrees.

> Do Not add any water
> Do Not cover with any lid
> Do Not salt outside of bird

BASTING

Well, do as you please. My most beautiful roast turkey last year won a New York State prize. I did not baste it once. It was glazed, golden, and gorgeous. The same day I heard a famous chef say he had basted a beautiful turkey every 15 minutes!

HOW-TO-DO TURKEY STUFFING

This stuffing is rich, flavorful, and just moist enough, but NOT crumbly. It definitely is *not* that green pasty kind that reeks with sage. This nice blend of thyme, sage, and sweet marjoram you will find delightful.

Thousands of new and not so new homemakers have adopted my turkey stuffing for a Thanksgiving regular and the glowing reports I've had are mighty gratifying.

You will need:

¾ to 1¼ cups good turkey stock

1 pint crusty corn bread (no sugar in it)

1½ quarts whole-wheat bread (2 or 3 days old)

2 eggs, slightly beaten

¾ cup melted butter or turkey fat

½ teaspoon each thyme, sage, and sweet marjoram

1 teaspoon salt

1 unpeeled apple, diced

¼ cup finely minced onion

¼ cup finely minced celery (inner stalks with leaves)

Handful unbroken pecan halves

1. Make stock before you start to clean turkey and let the stock simmer as long as you can, at least an hour, and 3 hours is better. I like to make it the day before and just let every smidgin of juice simmer out of the bones and meat. Use neck, gizzard, heart, and *feet*. I never bother to strain it, either. Why anyhow? Just discard the celery and seasonings. Lift out the bones and there's your rich stock plus turkey bits all cooked up in it.

2. Crumble corn bread or corn pone (pages 97, 167) into pieces, not too fine.

3. Crumble whole-wheat bread into small cubes about the size of a hazelnut. Leave crusts on bread. Don't toast it, but let it dry slightly in oven.

4. Beat eggs foamy and stir in melted butter and seasonings.

5. Use very largest mixing bowl and combine breads, diced apple, onion, celery, pecans.

6. Now add egg and seasoning mixture and stir well.

7. Begin adding stock and test carefully after you've added about ¾ cup. Mix with your hands. It's the best way.

My test: Pick up dressing and press it between your hands. Press gently, just so it holds together and does not pack. Now put it on a plate. If it holds together, but barely separates as you lift it with a fork, there is enough moisture. This is the way it will be when baked. Don't get it wet and pasty!

Fills a 15-pound turkey.

HOW-TO-DO TURKEY PASTE

You will need:

> 4 tablespoons butter
> 5 tablespoons flour
> 2 tablespoons lemon juice

1. Cream these 3 ingredients together until you have a smooth paste.

2. Rub breast and wings and all joints well with this paste. Put it on smoothly. No lumps or bumps. It will bake and keep the bird moist at the joints.
No, it doesn't taste at all.

ROASTING TIME FOR TURKEY

A temperature of 350 degrees roasts a perfect turkey. You need to know weight of stuffed turkey, time per pound, total cooking time.

POUNDS	MINUTES	HOURS
7	25	3
12	19	3¾
18	17	5
22	15	5½

How-to-do Broiler Chickens

1. Select broilers weighing from 1½ to 2½ pounds.
2. Split down the backbone.
3. Wash and pat dry.
4. Brush with melted butter and place skin side down on greased rack in broiler pan.
5. Place the pan so that the surface of chicken is about 4 inches below the broiler unit.
6. Broil at 350 degrees until browned and about half done.
7. Add salt and pepper. Turn and brush again with butter.
8. Broil until evenly cooked all the way to the bone. Small broilers require 30 to 40 minutes and larger ones need 40 to 50 minutes.

1½-pound broiler serves 2.

Serve hot, garnished with pickled peaches and spiced watermelon chunks.

How-to-do Long Island Roast Duck with Orange

This is a delicious serving, if excess fat is removed. I've never prepared this duck for guests who failed to ask HOW-TO-DO-IT. An oily taste is missing in my method and you have a moist, tender quality of duck with an orange sauce which is perfect.

1. Remove all down and feathers.

2. Clean inside of duck thoroughly. Be sure to remove every bit of organs along the backbone and clean and rinse inside well.

3. If there are large chunks of fat around the openings, cut them all off before roasting.

4. Rub inside lightly with salt and with ginger (1 teaspoon).

5. Now fill inside and neck openings with unpeeled apples, cut into quarters.

6. Fasten opening at lower end with toothpicks and lace them together, as you lace a shoe.

7. Next, fasten the neck portion tightly to the back of the duck, using a skewer.

8. Then run a skewer through the legs.

9. Now truss the duck into shape by running soft cord from the neck skewer to the leg skewer.

10. Bring the cord over to tie the legs securely in front.

11. Finally, place three slices of orange, rind and all, on the breast of the duck, fastening them with toothpicks.

12. Place on rack in shallow roasting pan.

13. Set into 425-degree (very hot) oven for 20 minutes. At the end of this 20 minutes' hot roasting the excess fat cooks out. So lift the duck out and pour off every drop of the fat.

14. Put duck back on rack and return to hot oven just long enough for surface to heat sizzling hot (about 5 minutes).

15. Now dash 1 cup unstrained orange juice all over duck.

16. Turn oven heat down to 325 degrees.

17. Roast until done, which means 1 hour and 20 minutes more for a 4-pound duck. This allows 20 minutes per pound after the fat is all poured off and the heat turned to 325 degrees. The sauce in the bottom of the pan is beautifully flavored.

Serves about 4.

FISH AND SEA FOOD

How-to-do Pan-fried Silver Smelts

At my favorite fish restaurant they serve these flavorful, crisp little silver smelts with tartar sauce and toasted French rolls, lightly sprinkled with Parmesan cheese. They are so easy to do and so delicious.

1. Cut opening about 2 inches long in lower side of fish. Clean inside, removing vein along the center bone, and rinse in cold water.

2. Dry well and dust with flour.

3. Dip into beaten egg mixed with 2 tablespoons cold water.

4. Then roll in sifted dry bread crumbs.

5. Fry in heavy skillet in about 1/4 inch hot fat.

6. Keep the heat moderate, as the delicate fish should not cook too fast.

7. As soon as browned and crisp, turn and brown the other side; then fish is done. Do not overcook.

8. Serve hot with wedge of lemon and tartar sauce (see page 148).

The gourmet eats the feathery bones and all. But if you don't care for the bones, they are easily removed all in one piece. Just split down the center of backbone and loosen gently with knife, then pull the backbone and all small bones loose and out.

How-to-do Poached Salmon

1. Buy 2 pounds fresh salmon.
2. Add salt and pepper, lightly. Sprinkle with lemon juice.
3. Wrap in cheesecloth or in parchment paper.
4. Drop into a pan with enough hot water to cover.
5. Add a few celery leaves, a bay leaf, a pinch of thyme, and a sprig or two of parsley.
6. Cook, covered, over *simmering* heat for about 20 minutes.
7. Take from water and remove cloth or parchment paper.
8. Pat dry and serve on heated platter.
9. Garnish with lemon wedges and pickle fans. Pass Remoulade sauce (page 163). (To make pickle fans, simply slice the pickle lengthwise from one end to the other, but do not cut through the stem end. Spread the slices apart fan-fashion.)

How-to-do Flounder Baked in Parchment Paper

This is a fine way to prepare fish to avoid the odor so often objected to and the fish is excellent, with all juices retained. Just remove paper when it is done, turning the juices out over the fish.

1. Clean flounder carefully and wipe dry.
2. Lay a piece of parchment paper flat on the table.
3. Rub the middle of the paper with butter and place the fish on this spot.
4. Be sure to salt fish lightly and sprinkle with lemon juice. Add one tablespoon of minced parsley.
5. Fold the paper tightly to make a seal and lay the paper-wrapped fish in a shallow pan.
6. Sprinkle lightly with water and bake in a 400-degree oven for 25 minutes.

NOTE: Parchment paper for cookery can be obtained at your household-goods store and is quite inexpensive. If carefully handled, it may be washed, dried, folded, and used again and again.

How-to-do Mountain Trout

Fat tender little trout from icy mountain water require almost no effort.

1. Clean the trout and roll it in meal.
2. Heat butter or salt-pork fat in a heavy skillet using just enough to prevent fish from sticking to pan.
3. Drop trout into skillet to brown over medium heat for only a few moments.
4. Turn and brown other side. Salt and pepper lightly.
5. Serve on heated plate right now. Add plenty of big lemon wedges.

NOTE: If you catch big speckled rainbows, lay strips of bacon over them and broil, but not too fast.

HOW-TO-DO FRESH SHRIMP

2 pounds shrimp
1 cup water

1 stalk celery and leaves
4 or 5 peppercorns

1. Bring water and seasonings to boiling point and add the 2 pounds of shrimp.
2. Cut the heat down and simmer, covered, for exactly 5 minutes.
3. Drain, cool, and remove the peel and the black line.

Shrimp cooked this way are done, but not overcooked. All the true flavor is retained and they are moist and delicious.

How-to-do Oysters Rockefeller

This is not an economy serving. But it's worth saving up for and if you are going to offer it, do it correctly. No substitutes please.

You will need:

2 dozen oysters on half shell
4 deep piepans filled with rock salt

1. Open oysters just before ready to prepare the serving. Leave them intact on the deeper shell. Be very careful not to lose any of the liquor around the oysters.
2. Settle ½ dozen oysters in the bed of salt and spread a very thin coating of rich Rockefeller Sauce over each oyster, sealing the mixture close to the edge of the shell.

3. Now place them in a hot oven, 400 degrees, for from 6 to 8 minutes.
4. Take them to the table right out of the oven, serving in the pans. They *must* be served HOT, or all the savory goodness is lost.

How-to-do Rockefeller Sauce

My friends in New Orleans make this sauce in quantities and keep it in the refrigerator all through the oyster season.

You will need:

2 cups fresh spinach
½ bunch anise
½ bunch scallions (young green onions)
2 tablespoons minced parsley
3 stalks Pascal celery
1 tablespoon anisette (Pernod may be used)
½ cup oyster liquor (approximately)
⅔ cup toasted bread crumbs, *sifted*
1 cup melted butter
Dash of Worcestershire sauce may be added

1. Run all vegetables through fine grinder or food chopper.
2. Add seasonings.
3. Stir in fine crumbs.
4. Now melt 1 cup butter and stir into the vegetables.
5. Last, stir in enough oyster liquor to make a saucelike mixture. It should *drop,* not pour, from the spoon as placed on the oysters.

How-to-do Fish and Chips

1. Buy fillet of haddock and cut each fillet into approximately 3 pieces. Be sure to cut them on the bias so edges are thin.

2. Using paper towels, pat fish dry.
3. Then dip (one piece at a time) into batter and fry in hot fat, 375 degrees,* for 3 minutes.
4. Drain on soft paper.
5. Serve piping hot with tartar sauce and French fried potatoes.

HOW-TO-DO BATTER

You will need:

2 cups all-purpose flour	1 egg
1 teaspoon salt	½ cup milk
½ teaspoon baking soda	½ cup water

1. Sift together flour, salt, and soda.
2. Beat egg until foamy. Add milk and water, mixed.
3. Stir well and quickly beat into the dry ingredients; unless batter is perfectly smooth, strain through wire sieve. Keeps for days, if covered, in refrigerator.

HOW-TO-DO TARTAR SAUCE

To one cup mayonnaise add 2 tablespoons each chopped sweet pickles, green olives, and capers and 2 teaspoons minced chives or onions.

HOW-TO-DO
BROILED SHRIMP IN CHILI SAUCE, WRAPPED IN BACON

This is one hot appetizer men go for. Delicious with drinks. Easy to prepare ahead of time and run under the broiler for a few minutes at the last. Make plenty.

* If you have no thermometer, a square of bread will brown in one minute if fat is 375 degrees.

You will need:

2 pounds freshly cooked
  cleaned shrimp
1 cup chili sauce

2 cloves garlic, chopped
1 pound paper-thin slices of
  bacon
Box round toothpicks

1. Dip cleaned fresh shrimp into the chili sauce, to which garlic has been added.
2. Broil bacon on one side only.
3. Cut bacon in half.
4. Wrap a half strip of bacon around each shrimp and fasten securely with a toothpick.
5. Place on a wire cake rack and broil until bacon is crisp and done all around.
6. Serve hot, holding with toothpicks.

VEGETABLES

How-to-do White Fluffy Rice

Cooking rice perfectly requires no skill. It is simply a matter of following the directions exactly as they are given. Of course, rice must be white and fluffy, with each grain standing apart.

1. Measure 1 cup long-grain rice.
2. Pour it into a sieve and run cold water through it for several minutes. Lift it up from the bottom occasionally and wash thoroughly.
3. Be sure that the water runs clear. Then you have washed all the starchy coating off.
4. In a heavy saucepan, heat 2 cups of water with ¼

teaspoon of salt. As soon as it boils, add the rice, stir, and let it come back to boiling.

5. Put a tight lid on and turn heat to low (I mean just as low as possible). It must simmer, not boil.

6. Simmer for exactly 15 minutes.

7. Remove lid and let all steam evaporate. This requires only about 5 minutes more. Do not stir. Using a fork, lift the rice gently away from the center of the pan once or twice to let all steam escape.

Makes 3 cups cooked rice.

This is dry whole-grain white rice. Add a chunk of butter and you are ready for rice and gravy, or Creole Rice, or a rice ring, or fried rice and many other good combinations you will work out for yourself.

How-to-do Fried Rice

A delicious serving for an emergency. Men like this, so declare an emergency frequently.

2 cups cooked rice (page 149)   2 pimientos, minced
4 tablespoons butter   4 tablespoons soy sauce
1 green pepper, shredded   4 eggs
1 bunch young green onions
  (scallions), finely sliced

1. 2 cups perfectly cooked rice (keep it hot).

2. Heat butter in heavy skillet. In it sauté shredded green pepper, onions, and pimientos. Cook gently about 10 minutes.

3. Add rice and soy sauce, stirring until well blended and hot.

4. Now beat the eggs until foamy and add to the seasoned rice in skillet.

5. Keep heat low and using a broad spatula—like a turner—fold eggs over to one side as they cook. Let uncooked portion run back to coat skillet and cook. Keep turning and mixing till moist and light. Taste and add more soy sauce if you like.

6. Serve immediately, if not sooner.

How-to-do Baked Potatoes

1. Select baking potatoes of even size, of course.

2. Scrub well, for you will want to eat the skins.

3. Rub melted fat lightly all over the skins.

4. Bake in hot oven, 400 degrees, 45 to 55 minutes. A few minutes before potatoes are done, reach into the oven and pierce each one with a fork, to permit the steam to escape.

5. The minute they are done, remove, turn a fork in opening to fluff the potato, and insert a chunk of butter. Serve now and add more butter when you aren't looking. Be sure there is a French pepper grinder on the table. Freshly ground black pepper and butter are all that's necessary.

How-to-do Maytime New Potatoes

1. Scrub new potatoes, but do not peel.

2. Cover with boiling salted water (1 teaspoon salt to each quart water).

3. Cook until tender.

4. Drain.

5. When potatoes are well drained, leave them in their pan and holding this pan of dry potatoes over medium heat shake gently, until potatoes are very dry and no moisture remains in pan.

6. Now add a generous chunk of butter and again shake the potatoes over medium heat until they are well coated and lightly browned. Turn into a heated dish and using the scissors, snip off chives to season them. Just plain good to eat!

How-to-do Mashed Potatoes

There is actually no excuse for lumpy, dry mashed potatoes. All you have to do is give them lots of hot milk and lots of beating.

1. Cook potatoes in plenty of rapidly boiling water.

2. As soon as they are done, drain them and hold the pan of potatoes over the heat as you shake them perfectly dry. This is important and too often slighted.

3. While they are piping hot, mash potatoes until free from lumps. Then pile them all to one side of the pan and holding the pan over low heat add milk and a chunk of butter, pouring it into the empty space in your pan. Let this milk heat.

4. Now, using a wire whisk, or even a fork, whip the potatoes until white and fluffy. If more milk is required, be sure to heat it before adding. Remember potatoes are starch and they absorb lots of milk. Add salt and pepper and serve.

How-to-do Buttered Yellow Squash

I hear friends say "Ugh, I can't stand squash." And then ask for seconds when I serve these.

1. Select *smallest* yellow squash.
2. Cook in tightly covered kettle, using small amount of water, just enough to prevent burning.
3. Cook *only* until tender. Drain well.
4. Add salt, a little sugar (less than 1 teaspoon), and lots of paprika.
5. Then add butter generously (when nobody is looking add more) and cover again to simmer gently 5 minutes over low heat.
6. Turn into sizzling hot bowl and serve piping hot!

It is the extravagant amount of butter simmered into them which makes them so good. I usually plan to go butterless the next day to ease my conscience. But they are worth it.

How-to-do Acorn Squash

These little winter squash are good with fish and this is a recipe I've used for years and I'm always asked for the recipe each time I serve these squash.

1. Cut the top slice from each squash and remove seeds.
2. Rub inside with butter and salt and coat with brown sugar.
3. Then fill the centers with finely diced apple; diced lemon, rind and all; brown sugar, and butter.

4. Pour 1/3 cup water in bottom of pan around squash.

5. Bake in 400-degree oven 1 hour. For 4 squash I used 2 apples, ½ lemon, 2 tablespoons brown sugar, and about 2 tablespoons butter.

Nice to bake for week-end menus and may be reheated any old time.

How-to-do Fresh Black-eyed Peas

Have you ever eaten black-eyed peas, fresh out of their shells? They should be cooked mellow and rich and tender, with lots of their delicious liquor to go with big squares of hot corn bread. New green onions, right out of the garden, and red ripe sliced tomatoes still warm from the vines should complete this feast. Makes you feel might sorry for folks who never taste food the hour it's harvested.

1. Pour 2 pounds of shelled black-eyed peas into a large, heavy pan and cover with warm water and heat to boiling.

2. Cover with tight lid and turn heat down to simmer.

3. Simmer about one hour and then add ½ teaspoon salt, plenty of black pepper, and 4 slices of bacon cut into bits, or about 1 cup smoked-ham bits. (Southwesterners add a tiny red-hot pepper, too.)

4. Add enough water to keep peas well covered and simmer for 1 hour more, or until tender. They should never be mushy and must not be watery, but should have plenty of their liquor or juice left.

Dried black-eyed peas are usually available and are

prepared the same way. Longer cooking time is required and sometimes I finish them in the oven stripped with broiled bacon slices.

HOW-TO-DO TEN MINUTE CABBAGE SHREDS

You will need:

1 small head cabbage
2 tablespoons ham or bacon drippings

½ cup milk or sour cream
Salt, pepper, paprika

1. Shred one small head of cabbage.

2. Melt drippings in a heavy skillet over moderate heat.

3. Turn the shredded cabbage into the skillet and add milk or sour cream.

4. Cover and let it simmer for 10 minutes. Add salt, pepper, and paprika and serve from a heated bowl.

How-to-do Cabbage Wedges and Bacon Bits

1. Cut a cabbage head into 5 sections.

2. Remove center.

3. Drop sections into a very large kettle of rapidly boiling water, to which salt has been added.

4. Cook uncovered for from 15 to 18 minutes.

5. Drain slightly and arrange spoke-fashion on a large heated chop plate.

6. Drip small amounts of hot ham or bacon fat over the sections and crumble crisply broiled hot bacon bits over them.

7. Serve very hot.

How-to-do a Vegetable Dinner

GREEN ASPARAGUS

1. First, remove all the toughened ends and snip off the small spikes which grow along the stalks and which may hold grains of sand.
2. Wash thoroughly.
3. Drop into boiling salted water and cook only until tender. If asparagus is fresh and tender, it should require no more than 12 to 15 minutes.
4. Lift from the water into a very hot bowl and add Quick Sauce.
5. Serve *now*.

Quick Sauce (Substitute for Hollandaise)

In a glass measuring cup, stir together ½ cup mayonnaise and two tablespoons lemon juice. Heat over hot but not boiling water, stirring frequently. Serve over hot asparagus.

EGGPLANT AND TOMATOES (AND PLENTY GOOD TOO!)

1. Peel one eggplant and cut into large chunks.
2. Sprinkle generously with salt and let stand at least 30 minutes.
3. Drain on soft paper.
4. Now roll in flour which has been salted and peppered and dusted well with paprika.
5. Quarter unpeeled tomatoes and salt lightly.
6. Heat about 1/3 cup olive oil and brown the eggplant all over.

7. Add tomatoes and cook until heated thoroughly.

8. Sprinkle with finely minced chives or parsley and serve piping hot. Parmesan cheese may be added if you like.

How-to-do Green Peas in Lettuce Nest
(From a French Kitchen)

Peas prepared this way have a brand new flavor and taste-thrill.

1. Line a heavy saucepan with outer lettuce leaves, dipped in and out of cold water.

2. Into this nest pour a package of frozen peas, or fresh peas.

3. Add 1/3 teaspoon salt, a pinch of sugar, and a slight dash of nutmeg. Add a generous chunk of butter.

4. Now dip more lettuce leaves into water and while they're dripping settle them over the peas, tucking them in carefully, so they'll steam undisturbed by any dry heat.

5. Put a tight lid on the saucepan and cook, simmering, about 20 minutes.

6. Turn the peas and all the beautifully flavored juice into a hot serving dish and serve piping hot. Throw lettuce leaves out, as all flavor is cooked away from them.

How-to-do Baked Stuffed Eggplant

This is a delicious serving and I'm always pleased to watch men eat every bite of it, *after* they've declared they do not like eggplant! On a hot day serve it well chilled,

for that's a nice surprise. I arrange it on a heavy frosted
glass plate and then settle the serving on a bed of cracked
ice on a coffee tray. Nice!

You will need:

1 large eggplant	⅓ cup parsley
½ pound sweet onions	⅓ cup olive oil
⅓ pound green pepper	½ teaspoon salt
½ pound tomatoes	Black pepper

1. Cut a large unpeeled eggplant into quarters. Sprinkle
   generously with salt. Let it stand 30 minutes or more.
   Drops of water form all over the surface and dark
   water will ooze out of the pieces.

2. Then rinse quickly in cold water and slit through the
   center lengthwise.

3. Fill the opening with these sautéed vegetables:

     ½ pound onions sliced paper-thin
     ⅓ pound green peppers cut in thin slivers

   Sauté the onions and green peppers in 1/3 cup of olive
oil, cooking gently until onions are golden-colored. Next
add:

   ½ pound paper-thin slices of tomato
   ⅓ cup parsley, minced
   ½ teaspoon salt and plenty of freshly ground black pepper

4. Cook 2 minutes more.

5. Now stuff the sautéed vegetables into the eggplant
   sections.

6. Place in baking dish. Pour about 1 cup of water
   around them and bake in 350-degree oven for 1 hour.

7. Serve piping hot, or icy cold.
   Serves 6 to 8.

SALADS AND SAUCES

HOW-TO-DO UNUSUAL LIME DRESSING

I found this delightfully flavored dressing at beautiful Old Cornell one summer. It is perfect on fruit salads.

You will need:

1 large lime
½ cup honey

2 eggs
½ cup whipped cream

1. Grate the rind of the lime and stir all its juice into the honey.
2. Using rotary beater, beat the eggs until light and foamy.
3. Beat the lime and honey mixture into the eggs.
4. Cook over hot water, stirring constantly, until thickened. It is almost clear and very heavy when done. Be sure to keep water simmering, never boiling.
5. When cold, fold in the whipped cream. It is delicious without the cream too.

Makes 1½ cups.

HOW-TO-DO CAESAR SALAD

You will need:

½ bunch chicory
½ bunch Boston lettuce
1 bunch endive
1 bunch romaine
½ cup plain olive oil
4 tablespoons garlic-flavored olive oil
Freshly ground black pepper and salt

Dash tabasco sauce
2 teaspoons Worcestershire sauce
1 cup freshly grated Parmesan cheese
1 raw egg, unbroken
½ cup lemon juice, unstrained
2½ cups hot toasted croutons

1. Have everything ready, but do not mix until just before serving. And don't pass up an opportunity to put on a real show as you mix this superb salad at the table.
2. Greens must be crisp and perfectly dry. Tear them into nice big bites and place in a large wooden bowl.
3. Slowly toss with all the plain olive oil and half of the garlic oil.
4. Add salt, pepper, tabasco, and Worcestershire sauce and the grated cheese.
5. Now break the egg right on top of the greens and drench it all with the lemon juice and pulp.
6. Toss all lightly but thoroughly until no trace of the egg is seen.
7. Quickly dip the hot croutons in and out of the remaining garlic oil and toss them through the greens. This should be done with a light hand. This salad must be served pronto. (No oil should be visible in the bottom of the bowl, so add the last portion of oil sparingly.)

Serves 8 to 10.

How-to-do Orange Onion Salad

It's fun to see guests' surprise at this salad. Invariably they'll say, "Well, you know, I thought that a crazy combination, but isn't it good!" Try it one time, will you?

1. Select large white sweet onions or the red Spanish onions if available. Slice very thin crosswise slices and separate them into circles.

2. Peel big heavy oranges, removing every particle of the white outer membrane. Cut them crosswise into thin slices and carefully remove seeds. Chill.

3. When ready to serve, place watercress on salad plate. Arrange crisp onion circles and chilled orange slices on the plate so they overlap. Use plenty of crisp onion circles, which give it a light, cool appearance.

4. Pass simple French dressing, to be ladled on lightly.

There's a delightful taste surprise in the combination of crisp onion rings and very ripe orange slices. When I find Temple oranges on the market this is our salad and everyone asks for repeats.

VARIATION: Sometimes I add avocado circles to this salad. Simply pull the skin off (don't peel), then cut around the seed in even slices. Slip loose from the seed and quickly sprinkle with lemon or lime juice to prevent discoloration. On the salad plate is a slice of orange, an avocado circle, and an onion circle. Nice. Mighty good to eat also.

How-to-do Salad Surprises

1. Select really tart juicy apples. Core, but do not peel. Cut into cubes, good bite size, and sprinkle with lime or lemon juice.

   Slice fresh kumquats into very thin slices, using peel and all, of course. Mix apple and kumquats. Arrange watercress on glass salad plates and add a generous amount of the fruit to each plate. Pass Cardinal Dressing or lime dressing—to be used sparingly. This is a delicious combination. Wonderful as an appetizer salad.

2. Place romaine leaves on glass salad plates. Arrange sections of grapefruit alternately with sections of avocado. Be generous. Add French, Cardinal, or lime dressing sparingly.

Now sprinkle lavishly with pomegranate seeds.

In persimmon time I always add sections of persimmons to this salad, for a real taste thrill. Use this for a dessert salad.

HOW-TO-DO HOLLANDAISE SAUCE

Hollandaise sauce is really easy to make, if you understand the directions and then follow them. Temperature is the only hazard you have in attaining certain success every time. The eggs and butter must be mixed over water that NEVER NEVER comes near boiling point. I find a round-bottomed bowl set into a pan of hot water seems to give the best results. Also, I like to place an asbestos mat under the pan of water. Watch the water and keep the heat low. Keep beating the mixture just as long as it is over the hot water, otherwise the egg yolk will stick or coat the bowl.

It is important to have the butter only lukewarm as it is added, or the mixture will separate.

Here is my Hollandaise sauce recipe, which I've made dozens of times. I've never had a failure with this recipe.

You will need:

4 egg yolks
⅛ teaspoon salt and a dash of cayenne
¼ teaspoon lemon juice

2 tablespoons tarragon vinegar
½ pound (1 cup) butter
1 tablespoon water

1. In a round-bottomed bowl, beat egg yolks until pale lemon-colored.

2. Add salt, lemon juice, and vinegar and stir together.

3. Melt butter over hot (not boiling) water and keep it warm—lukewarm.

4. Set bowl of ingredients over a pan of hot water. Keep heat *low*. Don't let bottom of bowl touch water. *Never* let water boil. Even the bowl is not too hot to handle. This low temperature is most important.

5. Now, using rotary beater, beat egg and vinegar mixture in a bowl, beating until smooth and thick. It has a rich, puffy appearance. This takes from 8 to 10 minutes.

6. When well thickened, begin to add the *warm* melted butter, a little at a time, beating constantly, but not hard.

7. Add a little butter and beat, then sprinkle in a little water and beat some more.

8. Continue adding warm butter and water and beating until butter is used.

9. Remove bowl from hot-water bath and serve warm.

10. This sauce may be reheated over warm water. It will not separate if you follow directions. Remember basic egg cookery—low temperature.

How-to-do Remoulade Sauce

1. To 1 cup mayonnaise add 3 or 4 sweet-sour pickles, very finely chopped, 1 tablespoon parsley, 1 tablespoon capers, a bit of fresh tarragon or chervil or both.

2. Stir these pungent seasonings through the mayonnaise, blending thoroughly. Serve with poached salmon. Delicious for cold salmon, too.

HOW-TO-DO BARBECUE SAUCE
(Excellent on ribs, chicken, or any meat)

You will need:

1 cup chili sauce
½ cup wine vinegar
1 teaspoon dry mustard
1 small onion, grated
4 tablespoons brown sugar
1 tablespoon paprika

1 teaspoon chili powder
1 teaspoon salt
1 teaspoon Worcestershire sauce
½ lemon, grated rind and juice

½ cup red wine

1. Measure ingredients into a saucepan.
2. Heat gently to simmering.
3. Simmer 15 minutes *(do not boil)*.

How-to-do White Sauce

Did you say "Well of all things! Everyone knows how-to-do white sauce." Sorry, but you'd be surprised.

To begin with, I'm talking about a rich, flavorful sauce which definitely does *not* taste floury. The flour and butter are cooked together until *done*. I can't be bothered with a double boiler for this and if directions are followed it is not necessary.

1. Into a heavy saucepan, measure 2 tablespoons butter. Place it over LOW heat. Using a wooden spoon, stir carefully to melt butter.
2. Next, add 2 tablespoons flour with ⅛ teaspoon salt,

keeping heat LOW. Stir to blend butter and flour to make a paste. This will be thick and almost dry, but keep stirring and cooking over LOW heat till it thins down and begins to bubble slightly. Now you have an emulsion.

3. If you are a beginner, this is a good time to stop and taste this flour and butter emulsion. Go ahead, it won't hurt you. Does it taste *cooked*, buttery, as if it had quality to it? Fine.

4. Now slowly add one cup COLD milk, stirring thoroughly. Heat may be increased some.

5. Cook and stir until thickened, smooth, and flavorful. Taste it again. Good stuff? Not a bit like most white sauce, which tastes exactly like library paste.

*   *   *

Having mastered excellent sauce, you are ready for beautiful cream soups, really good croquettes, creamed chipped beef—which is a poetic production—and many other fine servings. There are three sauces to be used:

LIGHT
2 tablespoons butter
2 tablespoons flour
1 cup milk

MEDIUM
3 tablespoons butter
2 tablespoons flour
1 cup milk

HEAVY
3 tablespoons butter
5 tablespoons flour
1 cup milk

Light sauce is for cream soups

Medium sauce is for creamed vegetables

fish

chipped beef

and similar servings

Heavy sauce is for croquettes and cutlets

Vary seasonings: minced parsley, onion juice, chives, nutmeg, curry, dill, and sherry wine. Use white pepper if sauce is to be perfectly white.

Always heat sauce bubbly hot when adding to vegetables or soup, so it doesn't thin down.

BREADS

HOW-TO-DO SPOON CORN BREAD

Arrange on a tray the following ingredients:

1 pint milk	1½ teaspoons salt
1 cup corn meal	4 eggs, separated

1. In heavy saucepan, heat milk to scalding.
2. Add meal, pouring in fine stream and stirring constantly to prevent lumps.
3. Add salt and cook over simmering heat until perfectly smooth, about 15 minutes.
4. Remove from heat and stir a minute to cool slightly. Then add egg yolks one at a time, beating rapidly.
5. In large bowl, beat egg whites until stiff, but not dry.
6. As soon as egg whites are beaten stiffly, *fold* them carefully through the mush mixture.
7. Turn into well-buttered 1½-quart Pyrex baking dish.
8. Bake 45 minutes in 400-degree oven.
   Serves 4.

How-to-do Crisp Corn Pone

My dad always said that he could tell when I made the corn pones for supper, because he recognized the prints of my fingers, and he would add that he thought them just a bit more crisp and golden on that account.

Even at ten or twelve years the eternal feminine responds to flattery, as he well knew, so I tried my level best to live up to his praise, thereby learning all the corn-meal tricks very early in my culinary experience.

I've often thought that if corn pones were called some plush name and featured by some haughty restaurant, they'd be famous all over the land.

1. Measure 2 cups white corn meal (water-ground meal if available). Don't sift, but stir ½ teaspoon salt into meal.

2. Quickly pour 1½ cups boiling water into meal, stirring rapidly to prevent lumping. This makes a very thick, heavy mush.

3. In a heavy skillet, heat 4 tablespoons shortening (I like half bacon or ham drippings).

4. When fat is sizzling hot—not smoking though—dip out a big tablespoon of mush, heaping full. It is very hot, so dip your hands into cold water and then press the spoon of stiff mush between your hands, letting your fingers make a deep imprint on each side. As you form the pones, place them in a skillet. Pones are the shape of an egg flattened out and are a little thicker in the center. Always place pones in the skillet so that they do not touch.

5. Fry, without moving them, until golden brown. Then turn and brown other side. Lift onto soft paper towel to drain a second before serving on hot plate.

Serves 4.

The browned, almost parched-corn taste of the corn pones is like no other delicacy. So good with green beans, salad, fish, or to crumble into a glass of rich cold milk.

I have made them very small and served them piping hot as an *hors d'oeuvre*. Never a smidgin left!

How-to-do French Bread—Flavorful and Piping Hot

1. Cut thick slices in a loaf of French bread, cutting just to, not through, the bottom crust.
2. Now cream 2 or 3 pats of butter till softened and add a little crushed garlic to it.
3. To a second bowl of creamed butter, add minced chives or minced parsley.
4. Spread each side of half of the slices with the garlic butter.
5. For those who like a milder touch, spread the other half of the loaf with the parsley or chives butter.
6. Wrap the loaf tightly in aluminum foil, or place in a tightly closed paper sack, and heat in 350-degree oven about 15 minutes.
7. Serve hot.

How-to-do Variations on Biscuits

NOTE: Basic recipe for biscuit dough on page 40.

1. Roll biscuit dough thin. Cut in large rounds. Place a

small piece of lump sugar soaked in orange juice on one half of the biscuit and place the other half over the sugar. Press edges together. Bake as usual.

2. Make biscuits by basic recipe, only add ¾ cup finely grated sharp cheese to dry ingredients. Cut into tiny biscuits and bake as usual. Serve piping hot.

3. Roll biscuit dough very thin in rectangular shape. Spread generously with melted butter. Cover with thick layer of brown sugar. Strew broken pecans over this. Roll from long side jelly-roll style. Seal edges by pressing tightly together. Cut in thick slices and place on oiled baking sheet. Bake as usual and serve HOT.

4. *Bites for Hors d'Oeuvres.* Add ¼ cup butter to shortening for basic recipe (page 40). Roll dough very thin and spread with melted butter. Cut biscuits with smallest cutter. Cover one round with paper-thin piece of baked ham. Place another round on top of ham. Press lightly together. Fill baking sheet with these and bake as usual. Serve hot right out of the oven.

5. *Drop Biscuits.* Follow basic recipe, but add enough milk to make a drop dough. Drop by spoonfuls onto oiled baking sheet. Just before they are done, poke a date, or a tiny hot sausage, or a cheese square, into the middle of the hot biscuit. Serve hot. Sometimes I add chopped dates, or plumped raisins, or crumbled bacon to the drop dough and bake as usual.

6. *Pin-wheel Biscuits.* Roll biscuit dough (page 40) very thin to form a rectangle; brush surface with melted

butter. Cut pimiento strips and green pepper shreds and scatter them over the sheet of dough. Begin with the long side and roll, jelly-roll fashion, pressing the long edge tightly to seal. Then cut into slices about 1½ inches thick. Pull apart slightly and lay, cut side down, on baking sheet so they do not touch. Bake in 400-degree oven about 20 minutes and place atop any meat pie or chicken pie, or even serve as is.

DESSERTS

HOW-TO-DO
OLD-FASHIONED STRAWBERRY SHORTCAKE

You can turn the plainest menu into a company dinner when you serve strawberry shortcake for dessert. And you need not wait for strawberry time, either, because frozen berries—and frozen peaches or apricots—are really luscious shortcake makings!

Just whisk together 2 layers of super-rich biscuit dough and put them into the oven to bake as you sit down to dinner. By dessert time, the shortcake is done and may be served piping hot.

You will need:

2 cups all-purpose flour	2 tablespoons sugar
4 teaspoons baking powder	½ cup shortening
½ teaspoon salt	⅔ to 1 cup rich milk
¼ teaspoon nutmeg	Strawberries, frozen or fresh

1. Sift and measure flour, baking powder, salt, nutmeg, and sugar. Sift into a mixing bowl.
2. Using pastry blender, chop shortening lightly into flour mixture.

3. Add enough milk to the flour mixture to make a very soft dough but not a sticky dough.

4. Add the rest of the milk gradually, stirring ONLY until ball of dough follows the fork around without sticking to the bowl. Don't stir any more than necessary.

5. Now turn the dough onto lightly-floured pastry cover and roll gently with covered rolling pin.

6. Roll to form an oval sheet of dough, very thin.

7. Cut into 2 round layers.

8. Fit 1 layer into a buttered 9-inch pie pan and brush it generously on top with melted butter.

9. Settle the other layer on top of that and brush it well all over with more melted butter.

10. Bake in 450-degree (hot) oven for from 20 to 25 minutes.

11. Remove and slip a long knife or spatula through the 2 layers to separate them.

12. Place 1 layer, cut side up, on a chop plate.

13. Drench with frozen strawberries and juice.

14. Top with second layer, cut side up.

15. Cover with more berries and juice.

16. Cut into wedge-shaped pieces and serve with rich yellow cream. Top with whole berries.

When using fresh strawberries, slice them and add sugar about one-half hour before using. Let them stand at room temperature, not in refrigerator.

How-to-do Individual Peach Shortcake

1. Make shortcake as directed for strawberry shortcake.
2. Roll very thin and cut with large cutter (an ice-tea glass is a good size).
3. Bake.
4. While hot, stack in twos, using plenty of butter between layers as well as on top.
5. Pile frozen sliced peaches between layers and drench the top with peaches and juice.
6. Serve in dessert plates. And pass the cream!

How-to-do Buttermilk Sherbet

Until you've made this dessert on a sizzling hot day, you'll never know how cooling, refreshing, and delicious it is. Just don't let the buttermilk trip you. Try it once. It's low in calories, too.

You will need:

1 quart good fresh buttermilk	1 Number 2 can crushed
2 lemons, juice and grated	pineapple
rind of both	2 cups sugar
2 stiffly beaten egg whites	

1. Mix in the order listed, folding whites through mixture carefully.
2. Turn into 2 trays of your refrigerator to freeze.
3. When it begins to freeze on the bottom and all around the sides, whip it thoroughly.
4. Return to trays and freeze.
5. Chill sherbet glasses before serving.

Very creamy, fluffy, and white and a tart, satisfying finale to any menu in hot weather.

Makes 1½ quarts.

HOW-TO-DO RED APPLE RINGS

These are delicious with ham, chicken, or just by themselves. Sometimes I offer a serving of three or four clear, red apple rings on a plate with a generous square of cream cheese. They dress up plain breakfast oatmeal so that everyone asks for seconds.

You will need:

2 cups sugar	Red fruit coloring
2½ cups water	4 red apples

1. In a large skillet, heat together sugar and water.
2. As soon as the sugar is completely dissolved, bring the sirup to a boil and cook until it spins a thread when dropped from the edge of the spoon.
3. Now add a few drops of red fruit coloring, making the sirup winy red.
4. Cut unpeeled red apples, which have been cored, into very thick slices crosswise.
5. Drop the apple rings into the hot sirup. Arrange the rings so that they touch but do not lap.
6. Let the sirup come to a good rounding boil and then reduce heat, simmering the apple slices until they are tender and clear and hold their shape.
7. These rings need to be turned frequently while simmering. I use a pancake turner and handle them very gently. They should be translucent and keep their

shape. If cooked too rapidly, they will go to pieces. It is important to use a skillet or a kettle with a large surface so the rings are not stacked.

How-to-do a Pineapple Centerpiece
(Which May Be Eaten!)

1. Using a sharp paring knife, cut around each eye of a pineapple, then let the knife blade sink in almost as far as it will cut, or to the hard center of the fruit.

2. Now pull the eyes out and with each one will come a delicious spear of the pineapple.

3. Arrange these spears around a mound of powdered sugar and serve for dessert or for a first course.

4. To make a beautiful centerpiece, cut all the eyes loose from the pineapple, but leave them in place. Set the pineapple on a copper tray. Strew whole strawberries, stems intact, around the pineapple and arrange talisman roses around the edge of the tray.

A border of blue cornflowers also makes a delightful finale for the tray, or use your own garden flowers.

HOW-TO-DO BAKED RHUBARB

This is a delightful pick-me-up in midwinter. When I serve it baked this way, guests *always* eat it up to the last drop, then scrape that last drop up as they ask for the recipe. I never fail to convert rhubarb haters with this dish.

> 1 pound rhubarb
> 1 cup sugar

1. Cut the rhubarb into 2-inch pieces, being very careful not to peel one bit of it. (The peel holds both the color and the shape of the rhubarb.)

2. Then place the rhubarb in a baking dish.

3. Pour the sugar over it. DO NOT ADD ANY WATER.

4. Cover with a tight lid. Bake 20 to 30 minutes in a 350-degree oven. Rhubarb will be in whole pieces, with a lovely ruby-red coloring. The juice will be deep red and rich in flavor.

Good to look at and very good to eat.

HOW-TO-DO CHERRY PUDDING SURPRISE

This pudding is inexpensive, easy to make, and mighty good to eat. It is a surprise because the batter is poured into the bottom of the pan and comes up on top of the cherries during the baking.

Pour into saucepan:

2 cups cherries
1 cup juice (if not enough juice add water to make 1 cup)
½ to ¾ cup sugar

Heat the juice and sugar to dissolve, then add the cherries and set aside to cool. If cherries are very sour, use ¾ cup sugar. If they are put up in heavy sirup, you may not need to add any sugar.

Batter

1. Arrange on tray:

2 tablespoons butter   1 cup flour
1 cup sugar   1 teaspoon baking powder
              ½ cup milk

2. To make this easy batter, mix the butter and the 1 cup sugar to a crumbly consistency.

3. Sift the flour and baking powder.

4. Add flour and baking-powder mixture alternately with the milk, beating well after each addition.

To Bake

1. Butter a baking dish and pour the batter into it. (Use 1 to 1½-quart size.)

2. Then right in on top of this batter pour the cherries and juice.

3. Bake in a moderate oven (350 degrees) for 40 minutes. The batter bakes up on top of the cherries and is a golden brown. The cherries and juice in the bottom bubble through and are luscious. Serve warm.

Serves 6 . . . maybe.

HOW-TO-DO PEACH MAPLE FRANGO

Frango is a Seattle special and is ambrosia come to earth. But the peaches must be mushy ripe. Lucky you, if there's a peach orchard where you can pick up sun-ripened, dead-ripe peaches nobody else is wise enough to want. If not, go hunting at your market 'long about closing time. (Bargains galore!)

Arrange following ingredients on tray:

3 egg yolks with a dash of salt	2 cups extra-ripe soft peaches
¼ cup maple sirup	mashed (or run through
1 teaspoon gelatin	food mill or ricer)
2 tablespoons cold water	1 cup whipped cream

1. Beat egg yolks until thick and pale lemon-colored.

2. Heat maple sirup and pour hot sirup into egg yolks, beating hard.

3. Turn this into double boiler over hot, but not boiling water and cook, stirring until mixture coats the spoon.

4. Soften gelatin in 2 tablespoons cold water and stir it into the hot mixture.

5. Pour this into bowl to cool.

6. When cool, add the sieved peaches.

7. Fold stiffly whipped cream into mixture.

8. Turn into trays to freeze WITHOUT STIRRING.

Get Ready to Make Meringue

Meringues are basically simple to make; however, many fail to follow directions, which *are* important. Here then are a few general pointers to assure success every time:

You will have difficulty and may fail to beat egg whites into stiff peaks . . .

1. If there is even a little grease in the bowl.

2. If there is even a little grease on the beater.

3. If there is a bit of the yolk in the white.

Make it a rule to wash and scald the mixing bowl and beater and wipe them dry with a fresh, clean tea towel. Do this just before you start to make meringue.

Separate yolk and white of egg, dropping yolk into one container and white into a saucer. Then pour white from saucer into a large bowl in which you beat meringue.

Never risk separating egg over meringue bowl. It's too easy to break a yolk, or an egg could be—well, bad!

Separate eggs. Measure sugar. Don't beat eggs until ready to use meringue and always bake meringue immediately after it is beaten.

Never let the meringue wait, after it is beaten to proper stiffness.

Never place meringue on hot pie filling.

Never beat meringue after it reaches the peak stage.

Never place meringue *under* broiler—always in oven.

Never let meringue cool in a draft.

Each little bubble is filled with air. Don't break them down.

Now again, repeating that rule about mastering basic cookery, when you master simple meringue there is no problem in making baked Alaska, or an omelet, or angelfood cake, or soufflés, because you already know how to handle "egg bubbles."

HOW-TO-DO MERINGUES

Do you want in on a secret? Well, if you'll make these meringues and keep them on hand for emergencies you can impress your in-laws beyond words. Second, you may keep them for weeks, so see how nonchalantly you place a meringue on top of crushed strawberries, top it with 2 whole ripe berries, and set a jug of cream beside this. Your guests think you've really spent the day preparing party food.

You will need:

4 egg whites	1 cup sugar
1 teaspoon cream of tartar	1 teaspoon vanilla

A few drops of almond extract

1. In a large bowl, beat the egg whites and cream of tartar with a wire whisk until they are stiff and will not move in the bowl.
2. Gradually add the sugar, beating all the time.
3. Continue beating until the mixture is really stiff and will stand in peaks on the whisk.
4. Add vanilla and a few drops of almond extract.
5. Drop by tablespoons onto a lightly oiled baking sheet. Leave plenty of room between meringues.
6. Bake in slow oven (300 degrees) for 1 hour.
7. Remove from oven and quickly place sheet on damp tea towel. Steam loosens the shells and they may be removed easily.

8 to 12 meringues.

If meringues are placed in the refrigerator for an hour or two or even longer, they will never be hard and gritty or become sticky. Store in a tight tin box and they will keep for days, or even for weeks, making a fine emergency dessert. Split and fill with ice cream and strawberries. Or with any fruit.

HOW-TO-DO ANGEL OR MERINGUE PIE

This is one of my favorite desserts and may be served with any fruit. I keep it on hand for week-end servings and it always makes a hit. It is easy to make, not expensive, and so pretty as well as being good to eat.

1. Arrange on a tray:

   4 egg whites
   ¼ teaspoon cream of tartar
   1 cup sugar

   Few drops vanilla and almond
   flavorings

2. Beat egg whites foamy.

3. Then add cream of tartar and beat until stiff points are formed.

4. If you haven't an electric mixer, use a wire whisk and a large bowl, for a wire whisk is much more easily managed than a rotary beater.

5. When stiff points are formed, begin adding sugar a little at a time, beating until sugar is dissolved and you don't hear the grains against the bowl.

6. Add flavorings.

7. Turn into deep piepan which has been lightly oiled and dusted with flour.

8. Bake in 300-degree oven for 30 minutes.

9. Place pan on wire cake cooler.

10. When cold, cut into pie-shape pieces and serve with any fruit. (The four yolks may be used for soft or baked custard. Or, did you ever poach egg yolks until hard, then drain them and grate them onto salads, vegetables, or casseroles? Easy as can be.)

HOW-TO-DO BAKED ALASKA

Here's one easy way to be sure of applause. Make baked Alaska and serve it to just anybody. Everyone always thinks it's the last word in culinary triumphs.

Now, may I be the first to assure you that there's simply

nothing to it? Don't ever admit this fact to anyone else though; what's the use?

After all, you can buy ice cream. You can make or buy a plain layer cake, either sponge or butter. Now if you've worked to this page on your basic problems of cookery of course you can make beautiful meringue. That's all there is to it—plus a few minutes' heat in the oven.

You will need:

1 layer of cake about 4 by 12 inches	4 egg whites
	8 tablespoons sugar
1 brick of ice cream (1 quart)	1/4 teaspoon cream of tartar
	Few drops almond flavoring

1. Cover a small bread board or a large chopping board with plain white typewriter paper (be sure the board will fit into your oven).

2. Place a sheet or layer of cake on this, leaving at least 1 or 2 inches around the edge.

3. Settle a brick of ice cream in the center of this cake. Any shape may be used, but the brick is fine.

4. Next, cover the ice cream thickly and generously with meringue (see page 184), spreading it quickly. Be very sure to cover every particle of cream, sealing the meringue right down against the cake. It is important to cover ice cream perfectly so that NO heat gets through.

5. Now place in a 400-degree hot oven and bake for only 8 minutes, or until evenly browned all over the top.

6. Remove from oven and slide onto a cold platter or a chop plate. Serve immediately.

7. Cut through the meringue, the ice cream, and the cake and lift to chilled dessert plate. Wipe knife on damp cloth each time.

Serves 6.

You see, the board, the paper, the cake, and the meringue are all insulators against heat; and the ice cream, if well frozen, hasn't a chance to melt in so brief a time.

You need NOT explain such boring details to guests, of course. Just smile and bow, as any artist always does.

PASTRY AND PIES

HOW-TO-DO STANDARD PASTRY FOR PIES

This is merely a step-by-step recipe for pastry. Unless you admit that you make light flaky pastry which is ALWAYS perfect, and no problem at all, study HOW-TO-DO PASTRY until it's your own thinking. Next, go into your kitchen and follow directions without a single hint of a hold-back. Do you know what will happen? You will suddenly discover how easy it actually is to make wonderful pastry and you'll never have another failure.

You will need:

⅔ cup shortening	6 tablespoons cold water
2 cups all-purpose flour	½ teaspoon salt

1. Cut shortening into flour and salt until mixture is like coarse meal.
2. Sprinkle in 6 tablespoons of cold water.
3. Stir lightly to mix.
4. Turn onto waxed paper.

5. With your hands, press against the waxed paper to form a ball of dough.

6. Cut dough into 2 parts.

7. Roll 1 part into thin round sheet.

8. If to be used for pie shell:

    a. Turn a narrow hem around edge, pressing on rim of pan.

    b. Flute the edge.

    c. Prick with a fork.

    d. Bake at 450 degrees for 15 minutes.

    e. Cool on wire cake cooler.

This amount makes 2 pie shells or 1 two-crust pie.

HOW-TO-DO LEMON PIE FILLING

You will need:

1 cup granulated sugar	1 tablespoon grated lemon rind
4 tablespoons cornstarch	
1½ cups cold water	3 egg yolks
4 tablespoons lemon juice	1 tablespoon butter

1. In a heavy saucepan, mix the sugar with the cornstarch.

2. Add water slowly to dry ingredients until perfectly blended.

3. Cook rapidly, stirring constantly until thick.

4. Then reduce the heat and cook slowly until thickened and clear as starch. It should drop in a heavy lump.

5. Now add lemon juice and grated lemon rind. Grate

only the thin yellow skin, or "zest" (no white portion). Cook only a minute or two.

6. Remove from heat and add a small portion of the hot sauce to 3 slightly beaten egg yolks.

7. Mix well and add all the yolks to the hot mixture.

8. Return to slow heat and stir well, cooking 3 minutes longer.

9. Stir in butter and set aside to cool (not in the refrigerator).

10. When cold, turn into cold pastry shell and top with meringue.

HOW-TO-DO MERINGUE FOR PIE

3 egg whites
6 tablespoons sugar
Dash of salt

1. Beat egg whites until stiff.

2. Sprinkle in sugar, adding only about 2 tablespoons at a time, and beating each time until every grain of sugar is dissolved.

3. Beat until very stiff peaks are formed.

4. Pile meringue unevenly on top of cold filling and seal closely against the pastry shell.

5. Sprinkle lightly with coconut.

6. Bake in 350-degree oven 15 minutes, or until a beautiful brown (oven—NOT broiler!) Cool on wire cake cooler, out of draft.

How-to-do Madelyn's Coconut Cream Pie

Best coconut pie I ever ate, and made beautifully by my pretty Southern sister-in-law.

1. Turn pastry (page 182) onto waxed paper.
2. With your hands, press against the waxed paper to form a ball of dough.
3. Roll to form a circle of thin dough.
4. Fit loosely into 9-inch piepan and turn a narrow hem around the edge of the pan, pressing the pastry onto the rim of the pan.
5. Flute the edge. Prick with a fork all over the surface of the bottom and side of the pan.
6. Bake in 450-degree oven for 15 minutes.
7. Cool on wire cake cooler.

FILLING

1. In a heavy saucepan stir together:

   ½ cup sugar   2 tablespoons cornstarch
   3 tablespoons flour   ¼ cup milk

2. Mix until smooth and stir in 1¾ cups milk.
3. Cook over moderate heat, stirring constantly, until it begins to thicken and bubble up. This takes about 10 minutes. Continue cooking 5 minutes longer, stirring occasionally.
4. Remove from heat.
5. Beat 3 egg yolks slightly and add a dash of salt, not more than ⅛ teaspoon. Now stir 4 or 5 tablespoons of the hot sauce into the egg yolks, adding a little at a

time and stirring as it is added. This prevents over-cooking the yolks to a curdle.

6. Then add all this to the hot sauce in your pan and cook over low heat for 2 minutes, stirring constantly.

Add 2 tablespoons butter, 1 teaspoon vanilla, and a few drops of almond flavoring. Stir in 1/3 cup shredded moist coconut and cool. When *cold,* turn into *cold* pastry shell and top with meringue (see recipe page 178).

How-to-do Custard Pie

This is the kind of custard pie which does NOT have a soggy crust or watery custard. It's smooth, velvety, and delicious, always.

HOW-TO-DO PASTRY

Maybe you need to study HOW-TO-DO PASTRY on page 182). But this is a special pastry.

1 cup all-purpose flour, sifted	1/3 cup shortening
1/2 teaspoon salt	1 whole egg, well beaten

1. Sift flour and salt together.
2. Cut shortening into flour until mixture is crumbly, like coarse corn meal. Don't *overmix.*
3. Now stir one whole well-beaten egg into the mixture and stir lightly until fairly well mixed.
4. Turn out onto a double thickness of waxed paper and press your hands against the paper around the dough to form a ball.
5. Chill in refrigerator for about 30 minutes if you have time. Not absolutely necessary, but it helps to handle the dough more easily.

6. Roll to fit a 9-inch piepan and settle the dough into the pan to fit closely.

7. Make a hem around the edge and then flute the edge. Do NOT prick the pastry as you usually do for a shell. Chill 20 minutes in refrigerator.

HOW-TO-DO CUSTARD FILLING

1. In a saucepan, mix 1/3 cup sugar with 5 teaspoons cornstarch and ⅛ teaspoon salt, and stir into it ½ cup milk.

2. Mix to form a smooth paste and add 2 cups more of milk, stirring well.

3. Stir this over moderately high heat until it barely comes to a boil. Don't let it boil.

4. Remove quickly and turn into a large bowl to cool.

5. Beat 3 eggs only until well mixed but not foamy.

6. Dip out 1 tablespoon of this beaten egg and pour it into the uncooked pie shell, rubbing it gently all over the bottom and sides of the pastry.

7. Then stir the remaining beaten eggs into the mixture.

8. Add 1 teaspoon vanilla and a few drops of almond flavoring.

HOW TO BAKE

1. Place the pastry in a preheated 350-degree oven and bake for 6 minutes. The surface of the shell will be well coated and the edge of pastry will be puffy.

2. Right at this second, reach into the oven and pour the custard filling into the shell. *Don't remove the pan to do this.*

3. Dust on top with nutmeg.

4. Bake for 30 minutes at 350 degrees.

5. All around the edge, the custard will be set, but the center will be soft. Test by slipping a silver knife into the custard in the center. A soft thick filling should cling to the knife. Don't wait for the knife to come out clean. However, ovens do vary and it may require from 5 to 10 minutes after the 30-minute test. Go easy, though.

6. Remove and set pie on a wire cake cooler to be really cold before cutting it.

COOKIES

HOW-TO-DO MAMA'S OATMEAL COOKIES

These are cookies I grew up on, so maybe that's why they are my favorite oatmeal cookies. They can't fail and are easy on the budget. Also, everyone from Grandmother to four-year-old Pixie can eat all he or she wants of these crisp, lacy-edged thin cookies.

You will need:

1 cup shortening	1 teaspoon cinnamon
1 cup sugar	1 teaspoon nutmeg
2 well-beaten eggs	4 tablespoons milk
2 cups flour	1 teaspoon lemon juice
1 teaspoon soda	1 teaspoon lemon rind
2 cups uncooked oatmeal	

1. Cream shortening and sugar together until light and fluffy.

2. Add beaten eggs and whip lightly.

Sift flour with soda and spices and add to egg, sugar,
nd shortening mixture. Beat well.

1 milk, lemon juice, and rind and beat again.

in oatmeal and mix thoroughly.

op by teaspoonfuls onto oiled cooky sheet. Leave a
ttle space between the cookies, as they spread.

7. Bake in 375-degree oven about 10 minutes. Remove
immediately and cool on wire cake rack.

HOW-TO-DO JELLY JEWEL COOKIES

These are simply delicious rich little cookies and they
keep indefinitely, so I store them in a tin box and offer
them for emergency fare. Easy to do and not expensive.

You will need:

½ cup butter (no substitutes if to be kept)
¼ cup brown sugar packed into cup
1 egg, separated
1 cup flour
1 cup ground pecans
Bright red jelly (currant or plum)

1. In a small deep bowl, cream butter and sugar until
puffy and light.
2. Stir in well-beaten egg yolk.
3. Add flour (no leavening at all, you see) and mix till
smooth. This is a soft dough and must be chilled at
least an hour before working with it.
4. Now, using a fork, beat the egg white slightly, just
enough to break it up.
5. When chilled, roll into balls about the size of large
marbles. Roll between palms of hands lightly.

6. Dip each ball first into egg white, then into mound of ground pecans.

7. Place on cooky sheet quite far apart.

8. Bake in 350-degree oven for 5 minutes.

9. Remove cooky sheet from oven and press the centers of hot cookies to form a depression. I use the end of the handle of a wooden spoon. Work quickly.

10. Return cookies to oven for 10 minutes longer.

11. Cool on wire cake rack and cut a tiny square of red currant jelly to drop into the center of each cooky.

HOW-TO-DO BERNICE'S SUGAR COOKIES

There was always a cooky jar filled with these crisp sugar cookies and all the children in the neighborhood knew the exact location of that cooky jar.

You will need:

¼ cup butter	1 teaspoon vanilla
1 cup sugar	2 cups flour (or enough more
3 eggs	or less to make soft dough
2 tablespoons milk	that will roll out)
2 teaspoons baking powder	

1. Cream butter and sugar until light and puffy.

2. Beat eggs until foamy and add milk and vanilla to them.

3. Sift flour with baking powder and a dash of salt.

4. Now beat the eggs into the butter and sugar mixture.

5. Add the dry ingredients, beating smooth.

6. Form into soft dough and chill at least half an hour in refrigerator.

7. Divide in 2 and roll ½ at a time, leaving other half to chill.

8. Roll on pastry cloth into very thin sheet. Be careful NOT to work any more flour into dough.

9. Sprinkle lightly on top with granulated sugar.

10. Cut into big-size cookies and place on cooky sheet.

11. Bake in hot oven, 450 degrees, for about 8 to 10 minutes, or until lightly browned.

CAKES, CAKE FILLINGS, AND FROSTINGS
HOW-TO-DO
LEMON CAKE WITH LEMON FILLING

My old-fashioned lemon cake is a delightful summertime cake. I make it for week-end fare and when we decide to have a hot-dog supper a wedge of fresh lemon cake turns the menu into a festive affair.

You will need:

¾ cup butter	2 teaspoons baking powder
1½ cups sugar	¼ teaspoon salt
4 eggs, separated	¾ cup sweet milk
2½ cups cake flour	1 teaspoon lemon juice
2 teaspoons grated lemon rind	

1. In a deep bowl, cream the butter until smooth and then cream the butter and sugar together till as puffy and light as whipped cream.

2. In small bowl, using a rotary beater, beat the egg yolks till they are thick and pale lemon-colored.

3. Add them to the butter and sugar mixture and beat again until thoroughly mixed.

4. Sift flour and measure correctly and then sift flour with baking powder and salt.

5. Add alternately with the milk to the butter and sugar mixture, beating after each addition. Continue beating until the batter is smooth.

6. Add lemon juice and grated rind and blend well.

7. Beat the egg whites until stiff, but not dry.

8. Gently fold the egg whites into the butter and sugar mixture.

9. Turn into 2 eight-inch round cake pans which have been lined on the bottom with oiled waxed paper.

10. Bake in 375-degree oven 20 to 25 minutes.

11. Set onto wire cake coolers for 5 minutes, then turn out.

12. Put together with lemon filling.

Tart Lemon Filling

You will need:

1 cup sugar	Juice and grated rind of 2
3 tablespoons cornstarch	large lemons
2 eggs	1 cup boiling water

1. Sift sugar with cornstarch.

2. Beat eggs with rotary beater until foamy.

3. Slowly stir eggs into dry ingredients and mix well.

4. Add juice and grated rind of lemons.

5. Stir in the boiling water.

6. Cook in double boiler, or over very low heat, stirring

constantly, until thick and smooth. It will be a very clear soft yellow and when cold will spread like jelly.

7. Let stand until cold and spread between and on top of two layers. Dust lightly on top with powdered sugar as pieces are served. Cut generous wedges and serve on plates with a fork.

HOW-TO-DO

SUSAN'S PERFECT WHITE COCONUT CAKE

This is my favorite of all the white cakes I've ever eaten. No substitutes are recommended. I'm glad to share its perfection with you.

1. Get ready. Arrange on a tray:

½ cup butter	½ cup milk
1½ cups sugar	½ cup water
3 cups sifted cake flour	1 teaspoon vanilla
3 teaspoons baking powder	¼ teaspoon almond extract
¼ teaspoon salt	4 egg whites

2. In mixing bowl, cream butter and sugar until mixture is as fluffy as whipped cream.

3. Sift flour with baking powder and salt and add about 4 tablespoons of it to the butter and sugar mixture.

4. Beat well, as this keeps butter and sugar from separating.

5. Then add the remaining flour, alternately with the liquid, beating after each addition. Add about ½ cup flour each time and about ¼ of the water each time.

6. Add extracts.

7. Beat the egg whites until stiff but *not dry*. They should still slip in the bowl as you tilt it, and be moist.

8. Carefully fold them into the batter.

9. Turn batter into 2 eight-inch round cake pans.

10. Bake in moderately hot oven, 375 degrees, for from 25 to 30 minutes, or until top of layer cake comes back evenly when you dent it with a finger to test.

11. Turn out onto wire cake cooler.

12. When cool, ice and shower long moist shreds of grated coconut all over the top and sides. On special days, I grate fresh coconut for this cake. Then I use coconut milk instead of the ½ cup of water in my recipe and leave out 4 tablespoons of sugar. If you use fresh coconut, change your recipe to read:

> ½ cup coconut milk
> ½ cup sweet milk
> 1¼ cups sugar

Then follow the rest of the recipe as it is.

HOW-TO-DO MY DATE CAKE

This grand old cake is truly educated, for it's gone to girls and boys away at school for years. A moist, delicious cake, easy to make and on the economical side. Will keep and grows better with time. Don't substitute, as it needs the butter for long keeping quality.

You will need:

3 cups flour	1 cup pecans
1½ teaspoons soda	2 cups fresh buttermilk
2 teaspoons each allspice, cinnamon, and nutmeg	½ cup butter
1 package dates, cut into strips	2 cups sugar
	1 teaspoon vanilla
	A few drops almond extract

½ teaspoon salt

1. Line the bottom of a 9-inch square pan, 2½ inches deep, with oiled brown paper.

2. Sift half of the flour with the soda and spices.

3. Sift remaining half onto a square of waxed paper and dust the dates and nuts in it, shaking them free from all but a light coating of flour (this is called "dredging in flour").

4. Heat the buttermilk until lukewarm, but NOT hot.

5. In a large mixing bowl, cream the butter and sugar together until light and puffy.

6. Add flavoring and a small amount of the flour (about 4 tablespoons), mixing well.

7. Now add flour and buttermilk alternately, beating well until smooth. A wooden spoon does a good job if you do not have an electric mixer.

8. Add dates and nuts, together with all the remaining flour which does not cling to them.

9. Turn batter into pan and bake in a moderate oven, 350 degrees, for 45 minutes.

10. Set on wire rack to cool about 8 minutes. Turn out on rack and remove paper from bottom.

11. Serve plain or ice with Quick Caramel Icing (page 103).

HOW-TO-DO ALLILU'S LAZY DAISY CAKE

You will need:

2 eggs	½ cup scalded milk
1 cup sugar	1 tablespoon butter
1 cup cake flour	¼ teaspoon almond extract
1 teaspoon baking powder	Dash salt

1. Break eggs in a deep bowl and beat with rotary beater until light and foamy.

2. Add sugar gradually, beating constantly.

3. Sift flour, baking powder, and salt together and add slowly, beating until smooth.

4. Scald the milk and butter together and while still hot

5. Add it to batter, giving it about a dozen more beats. Stir in almond extract.

6. Line bottom of 7½ x 11 pan with oiled waxed paper.

7. Turn cake into pan and bake in moderate, 350-degree, oven for 25 to 30 minutes, or until top of cake springs back evenly when lightly touched with fingers.

8. When cake is done, remove from oven and spread with following icing:

> In saucepan, heat 5 tablespoons butter with 4 tablespoons cream and ½ cup brown sugar (tightly packed in cup). Keep heat very low and stir carefully until sugar is dissolved. Remove from heat and stir in ½ cup coconut and ½ cup broken pecans.

9. Pour over warm cake in cake pan, spread smoothly, and run under broiler until golden brown and bubbly. Do not place it too close to broiler and watch closely, as it burns easily. Cut in squares and serve warm.

Mighty good cake and it's been an old standby in Allilu's home for twenty years.

HOW-TO-DO RED EARTH CAKE

You will need:

½ cup shortening	2 tablespoons strong hot coffee
1½ cups sugar	2 cups cake flour
1 egg	1 teaspoon salt
4 tablespoons cocoa	1 teaspoon soda
1 teaspoon red food coloring	1 cup fresh buttermilk
1 teaspoon vanilla	

1. Cream shortening and sugar until light and fluffy.
2. Blend in the egg, which has been beaten until light and foamy.
3. Mix cocoa, coloring, and hot coffee to a smooth paste. Stir into mixture.
4. Sift flour and measure, then sift again with salt and soda.
5. Add to mixture alternately with the buttermilk, folding and beating lightly after each addition.
6. Add vanilla.
7. Turn into 2 eight-inch pans, 2 inches deep, lined on the bottom with oiled waxed paper.
8. Bake in moderate oven, 375 degrees, 30 to 35 minutes.

Top with chocolate or caramel icing (pages 201, 103).

HOW-TO-DO SUSAN'S ANGEL FOOD CAKE

You will need:

1 cup sifted cake flour
1½ cups sugar
¼ teaspoon salt
1 cup egg white and 1 egg white more

1½ teaspoons cream of tartar
1 teaspoon vanilla
½ teaspoon almond extract

1. Sift flour once and measure.

2. Sift and measure sugar.

3. Separate eggs and measure 1 cupful of egg whites. Then run the cup over with 1 more egg white. Add cream of tartar.

4. In a very large bowl, using a flat wire whisk, beat the whites until stiff but not dry.

5. Fold in sugar, adding only a small amount at a time. Fold by carefully cutting down through, across, up, and over the mixture. Don't beat.

6. Add flour the same way. I like a large slotted metal spoon for this job. You may also find that a long-handled plate scraper does a good job for you.

7. Add vanilla and almond last.

8. Turn into an ungreased 10-inch tube pan. Gently slip batter out of bowl. Don't stir or beat it out, breaking down egg whites.

9. Bake in 325-degree oven for 1 hour.

10. Remove from oven and turn upside down to hang in pan till cold.

Serve with ice cream drenched with crushed strawberries and big cups of coffee, or ice with orange glaze (page 201).

NOTE: I use a very large bowl and a flat wire whisk when beating the egg whites. Fold gently and make each motion count when adding sugar and flour. DO NOT BEAT. DO NOT COOL CAKE IN A DRAFT.

HOW-TO-DO CREAM PUFFS

Cream puffs are really so easy to make and they are so good for all kinds of emergency fare, from main-course servings to desserts, that we should all master the few tricks about making them.

1. Arrange on a tray:

1 cup water	1 cup flour, sifted
½ cup butter	¼ teaspoon salt
	4 eggs, unbeaten

2. Add butter and salt to water in a saucepan and let this come to a boil.

3. When it is bubbling, just *dump* all the flour in at one time and stir rapidly until mixture thickens and leaves the sides of the pan, forming a ball of soft dough.

4. Remove from the fire and beat about 20 strokes with a wooden spoon.

5. Now add the unbeaten eggs, one at a time, beating thoroughly after each addition until the mixture be-

comes smooth again. Don't worry if the batter separates, for it will soon smooth out as you heat and it will be a velvety smooth and golden yellow drop-dough when finished.

6. Drop by tablespoonfuls onto lightly oiled cooky sheet.

7. Form high in the center and leave plenty of space between puffs, as they spread while baking.

8. Bake in 400-degree oven for 35 minutes.

9. Cool on wire cake rack.

10. When cold, slit on the side and fill with cream filling, or with fruit and whipped cream or ice cream, or with pudding mix.

11. Dust on top with powdered sugar.

HOW-TO-DO REFRIGERATOR FROSTING

This is always in my refrigerator and is really a pretty quick frosting for everyday cakes.

½ cup white corn sirup
1 egg white, unbeaten

1. Place corn sirup and unbeaten egg whites together in a deep bowl and using rotary beater beat until mixture stands in stiff points.

2. Add 1 teaspoon vanilla or almond, or 1 teaspoon fresh lemon juice with the grated rind, and stir well.

This icing may be poured into a refrigerator bowl, covered, and kept for days. Stir lightly again with a fork before using.

HOW-TO-DO FUDGE FROSTING

You will need:

2 cups sugar
2 squares unsweetened
chocolate

2 tablespoons corn sirup
⅔ cup top milk (or cream)
2 tablespoons butter

1 teaspoon vanilla

1. Melt chocolate. Add sugar, corn sirup, and milk or cream.
2. Stir over low heat until sugar is all dissolved.
3. Continue cooking slowly until mixture forms a soft ball when tested in cold water.
4. Remove from fire and let cool to lukewarm. Add butter and vanilla.
5. Beat until right to spread. This should not be as firm as fudge, but soft and creamy.

HOW-TO-DO ORANGE GLAZE

I make up a cupful or a quart of this orange glaze, because it's so good on so many servings. Cover well and keep in refrigerator for an emergency topping on hot gingerbread, apple dumplings, or even on stale cake warmed in the oven.

2 cups confectioners' sugar
1 tablespoon butter heated
quickly to brown lightly

½ cup orange juice
Finely grated rind of 1 orange

Beat well and spread on cool cake.

HOW-TO-DO
LEA AND LEE'S APPLESAUCE SQUARES

This is a delicious dessert serving for your television guests, afternoon, evening, or any other time, and it's so easy on the budget and so easy to do.

You will need:

½ cup shortening	2 cups flour
1 cup brown sugar	3 teaspoons baking powder
½ cup white sugar	¼ teaspoon salt
2 eggs	¼ teaspoon cinnamon

1 cup applesauce

1. Cream the shortening, the white, and the brown sugar together until it makes a puffy, creamy mixture.

2. Next add unbeaten eggs one at a time, beating well after each addition.

3. Sift together 2 cups of flour, 3 teaspoons baking powder, ¼ teaspoon salt, ¼ teaspoon cinnamon.

4. To shortening, sugar, and egg mixture add flour mixture alternately with applesauce, beating lightly after each addition.

5. Turn into well-greased jelly-roll pan, 15 x 11 inches.

6. Bake in 375-degree oven for from 20 to 25 minutes.

7. Cut into squares and serve warm.

Sometimes I spread the sheet lightly with orange glaze (page 201).

HOW-TO-DO POUND CAKE

You will need:

1 cup butter	¼ teaspoon salt
1⅔ cups sugar	1 teaspoon vanilla
5 whole eggs	1 teaspoon lemon juice
2 cups cake flour	Grated rind of ½ lemon

1. Cream butter, then cream butter and sugar, until as light and puffy as whipped cream.

2. Next, add the eggs, one at a time, beating hard after each addition. Do not add another egg until batter is smooth and fluffy each time.

3. Sift flour and measure, then sift again with salt.

4. Add in about 4 portions, folding and beating. Do not stir or overbeat, simply stop when batter is smooth and has absorbed dry ingredients.

5. Add flavorings and turn into oiled loaf pan, or a spring mold with a tube center is perfect for this cake (Line bottom of pan with oiled wax paper). Bake at 350 degrees for 50 minutes.

4. "The Little Meal"—
Supper, Brunch, Lunch

The kind of meal planning we do today makes supper, brunch, and lunch conform to pretty much the same pattern of menu making. On holidays, Sundays, and days off, when the family breakfasts late so that lunch and breakfast blend into one, we call the mid-morning meal "brunch." This is a meal built around one good main dish, with fruit or a vegetable (often raw) served either at the beginning or the ending of the meal as an appetizer. The dishes for brunch usually strike some decorative note which adds appetite appeal to the meal and sets a tone for leisurely enjoyment of a social, festive table.

Company luncheon follows the same meal planning pattern as brunch and so, too, does supper. But even a soup and a sandwich lunch for the homemaker at home alone fits into this pattern. A half grapefruit or fresh grapes may begin or end the lunch. The sandwich may be a date and nutbread one, with cheese and jelly filling. A glass of milk would make this a lunch to please the most exacting nutritionist (and the most careless non-nutritionist, who insists only that food must taste good).

Emphasis on these meals is simplicity. Just one or two well-prepared dishes as the center of attraction. Following a basic plan for one-dish meals, if you will master a few casserole dishes, learn one or two salads which are really good and perfect several interesting desserts . . . why you're in business!

Take, for instance, the recipe I have given you on page 209 for Cécile's Cheese Stuffed Tomatoes. You can serve these elegant tomatoes to five or to fifty. Once you have learned how to do them you can make them almost without a second thought. They are interesting, different, and filling enough to make a main dish (you can serve two to a person, if you wish). Moreover, when tomatoes are in season, they are thrifty as well as eye-filling. What more could one ask?

Learn How-to-do Chicken Paprika, page 241. There is a dish you will serve over and over again. Begin with a good salad and add fruit or a dessert at the end. Your menu may be as simple or as fancy as you wish.

In addition to such specific How-to-do dishes, which you can master for the preparation of this "little" meal, there are other basic preparations that are important to know well. Think of the dishes you can prepare from a beautifully simmered chicken. There's lots of meat on one chicken, sufficient to serve salad to a crowd; to make several chicken pies, if a number are to be fed. Club sandwiches can fit into the budget, if you get that chicken and cook it at home. You'll find the recipe for this basic How-to-do Simmered Chicken, page 240. This will really put you in business for Sunday-night visitors.

A buffet supper fits into this basic pattern just as well as a simple lunch. Learn How-to-do Roast Long Island Duckling with Orange Sauce, page 141. Roast it ahead of time for the buffet table and then serve it with a beautiful fruit salad and a simmering pot of your favorite soup. You'll find several such delicious soups beginning on page 228.

You've learned to make lemon meringue pie, page 183? Now turn this into little tartlets for the supper table, for buffet serving, or for that bridge luncheon.

This, then, is the pattern for "the little meal," whether served at midmorning, at noon, or in the evening. This meal allows more time for planning than do most breakfasts. It borrows dishes freely from other menus of the day. But it keeps those dishes simple and attractive.

HOW-TO-DO
MENUS FOR THE LITTLE MEAL

A thousand times a season I receive letters from my home-makers starting *The club meets at my house next time and I want something* different. *Now we are limited to* one *serving and a drink. We can have olives and stuff like that but nothing more. What?* This section, I hope, will be a little How-to-do for all such problem occasions.

- for a bridge-supper serving
- or a bridge luncheon on a cold day
- or a snack any time
- or On-your-plate

Tureen Filled with Chicken Velvet Soup (page 210)
Fresh Fruit Salad with
Pot Cheese
Melba Toast   Sweet Butter
Celery
Square of Hot Gingerbread (page 106)

A Festive On-your-plate

Chill this plate.

In the center, a thick circle of fresh, very ripe pineapple
On top of the pineapple a circle of ripe peeled avocado
    dipped in pineapple juice
On one side of the plate a mound of red raspberries
On the other side of the plate a cluster of chilled Thomp-
    son seedless grapes
Pass cloverleaf rolls and sweet butter with wild plum jelly
Serve iced coffee

A Simple On-your-plate

Poached Salmon (page 144)
Thick Wedges Red Ripe Tomatoes
Hot Potato Chips
Pickled Peaches
Crisp Cookies
Iced Tea

HELP YOURSELF SUPPER

(on Snack Bar, or on Breakfast Room Table)

1.

Tureen of Split Pea Soup
Tray of Melba Toast, Rye Toast, and Italian Bread Sticks
Big Bowl of Cooked Vegetable Salad
Baked Alaska (page 180)
Hot Spiced Cider

2.

Chile con Queso (page 218)
Relish Tray Filled with
Carrot Strips Sprinkled with Celery Salt,
Radishes, Cucumber Sticks Sprinkled with Lime Juice,
Italian Olives, Finochio (or Fennel), Wedges of Cantaloupe
Bowl Poached Fruit (page 39)
Coffee (page 33)

PATTERNS FOR THE LITTLE MEAL

1.

On-your-plate

Two Cheese Stuffed Tomatoes, Hot (page 209)
My Special Potato Salad in Lettuce Cup (page 242)
1 Celery Heart   3 Ripe Black Olives
Small Watercress Bread and Butter Sandwich

2.

On-your-plate

Jane's June Supper when meat is high and humidity
is higher.

Chilled Canned Vichysoisse
Toasted Buns, Buttered and Sprinkled with Sesame Seed
Radishes and Celery or Fennel
Lobster Chunks, Cold
or
Lobster Chunks Sautéed
Fruit

3.

On-your-plate

Chicken Paprika (page 241)
Maytime Potatoes (page 151)
Apple and Kumquat Salad in Lettuce Cup
Hot Corn Pone (page 167)
Coffee

There's nothing like a help-yourself supper when the group grows and time shrinks. Here's a lifesaver when you happen to have a big pie or cake or any bountiful dessert on hand.

Hot Cream of Pea Soup
Jellied Consommé with Thin Lime Slice (Summer)
Caesar Salad (page 159)
Salt Rye Toast, Buttered
Anna Maude's Pecan Pie (page 211)
Hot Coffee or Iced Tea

A GRAB BAG OF DISHES
FOR THE LITTLE MEAL

HOW-TO-DO
CÉCILE'S CHEESE STUFFED TOMATOES

These unusually seasoned baked tomatoes add that surprise note to your menu and they are so easy to do.

You will need:

6 medium-sized ripe tomatoes   ⅓ cup finely grated cheese
1 cup rusk crumbs   1 teaspoon paprika
          ⅛ teaspoon cayenne pepper

1. Select ripe, even-sized tomatoes and skin them (hold over flame or electric unit until the skins pop, then slip skins off quickly).

2. Cut a thick slice off the top and, using a spoon, hollow out the inside, leaving a thick shell.

3. Dust the inside with salt and freshly ground black pepper and turn upside down to drain while mixing the stuffing.

4. Grate rusks, or other very fine dry bread crumbs (but *fine*) to make a cupful and mix with grated cheese, paprika, and cayenne pepper. Stir until well mixed and add just enough melted butter to hold the stuffing together. Amount depends on the crumbs and the quality of the cheese.

5. Fill drained tomato shells, not pressing mixture tightly at all.

6. Set in shallow Pyrex baking dish and place in hot oven, 400 degrees, to bake for only 10 minutes. (Be sure to use oven, not broiler.) Serve hot.

Serves 6.

NOTE: The tomato pulp hollowed out is to be saved for soup or for sauce tomorrow.

HOW-TO-DO CHICKEN VELVET SOUP

This recipe was on my desk for months before I ever tried it. After I served it one time we adopted it as our most special soup. Chicken Velvet and my beautiful minced clam soup are the nicest soups I've ever tasted.

You will need:

1 quart good strong chicken
  stock *
2 tablespoons cornstarch
  mixed with a little cold
  water to make a paste

1 cup cream
4 egg yolks beaten till thick
  and pale lemon-colored

1. Stir cornstarch paste into chicken stock and cook slowly, stirring carefully until the raw taste is gone and the soup is smooth.

2. Add cream and let mixture come to boiling point, but do not boil.

3. Be sure egg yolks are well beaten as directed. Dip about 1 cup of the hot soup into the egg yolks and stir rapidly (this prevents overcooking the yolks).

4. Now pour yolk mixture back into soup and stir rapidly over LOW heat, cooking for about 4 minutes. Add a dash of nutmeg.

5. Serve in heated bowls, and top with 1 teaspoon whipped cream with a leaf of watercress in the center.

Serves 4 to 6.

'Tis like pale yellow chiffon velvet, or melted ivory, or liquid rainbows—and mighty good to eat.

HOW-TO-DO ANNA MAUDE'S PECAN PIE

You will need:

½ cup sugar
1 cup dark corn sirup
3 eggs

4 tablespoons butter
1 teaspoon vanilla
1 cup broken pecans

* The liquor in which a fat hen or fowl is simmered until done. Use the meat for chicken pie, salad, or club sandwiches.

1. Line a 9-inch pie plate with pastry (see page 182) and flute the edge.
2. Place sugar and corn sirup in a saucepan and cook till mixture thickens. This is 228 degrees on thermometer and an even 10 degrees below the thread stage.
3. In a deep bowl, using a rotary beater or an electric beater, beat the eggs until light and foamy.
4. Now add the hot sirup to the eggs and beat well.
5. Stir in the butter, vanilla, and nutmeats (save a few for the top). Pour into unbaked pie shell. Strew a handful of pecan halves over the top.
6. Bake in a moderate oven, 350 degrees, for from 50 to 60 minutes.
7. Place on wire cake rack to get cold before cutting.

Wonderful!

HOW-TO-DO FRANK'S CHEESE SUPPER

This is such a nice supper serving when there's little time to plan or market for a menu. Add a green salad with Cardinal Dressing (page 76) and a perfect fruit dessert and there is nothing missing but the coffee.

You will need:

6 slices bread	Paprika
4 tablespoons butter or margarine, melted	4 eggs
	¼ teaspoon salt
Minced chives	Pinch dry mustard
1 pound Cheddar	3 cups milk

1. Butter generously your largest oblong Pyrex baking dish.

2. Place slices of bread on the bottom of the dish.
3. Brush each slice with melted butter and sprinkle with finely minced chives.
4. Cover with a thin slice of Cheddar cheese and top the cheese with another slice of bread.
5. Brush the bread with melted butter and sprinkle grated cheese over the top, dusting lightly with paprika.
6. Beat eggs slightly. Add salt, a pinch of dry mustard, and milk. Stir well.
7. Pour very slowly over the bread and cheese, stopping at each portion to let the custard soak into the bread.
8. Bake in a moderately slow oven, 325 degrees, for 50 minutes. Increase the heat to about 400 for 5 minutes to get that rich golden glaze on top. Serve right now, or sooner.

Here's a puffy, nourishing cheese-custard sandwich which is not only good for you but lickin' good besides. Make individual servings of this by using sliced toasted buns in individual pottery baking dishes. With a fruit salad of good raw fruit this can be a wonderful one-dish luncheon.

HOW-TO-DO
SOUTHWESTERN CHILE CON CARNE

It seems to me that everyone should just naturally like chile. But I've learned that growing up on chile and hot tamales has a lot to do with this taste. Being able to get *good* chile is even more important. In fact, chile just has to be good. Here's the way.

214 : A GRAB BAG OF DISHES

You will need:

2 lbs. beef shoulder	2 teaspoons comino seed
¼ lb. suet	(cumin)
2 cloves garlic, finely minced	2 chili peppers, sieved
3 tablespoons chile powder	1½ cups hot water
2 teaspoons salt	Pink beans (cooked)

1. Cut beef shoulder into very small cubes (I do not like it ground, but want it finely diced).

2. In a heavy skillet, fry out the suet, cooking over moderately high heat until pieces are crusty brown. Don't burn.

3. Sprinkle in finely minced garlic, stirring to cook well.

4. Now add meat, turning and browning.

5. Stir in chile powder, salt, comino seed, and chili peppers.*

6. Add 1½ cups hot water. Cover with good tight lid and simmer for 2½ hours. Stir 2 or 3 times.

7. Add 1 cup more hot water and simmer about 30 minutes longer, or until meat is perfectly tender.

8. Add pink beans well cooked and seasoned with salt, black pepper, and chile powder

A Good Chile Supper for Six

Chile con Carne con Frijoles
(Chile with Meat and Pink Beans)

Hot Tamales	Crisp Fried Tortillas
Fresh Pineapple	Black Coffee

* Every Mexican home and all Southwestern markets have a string of shiny dark red chili peppers hanging beside the back door to dry. To use them, simmer or steam until puffed up as they were when green, or freshly picked from the vines. Remove seeds and press through coarse sieve. Use this pungent pulp in chile.

How-to-do a Clambake . . . at Home

You can have this wonderful clambake right in your own house or apartment. Or you can prepare the feast in your kitchen and take it in your car to the beach or on a picnic. This is a prized recipe, carefully worked out by Mr. Royal Toner, Chairman of the Public Relations Committee of the Oyster Institute of North America, President of the National Fisheries Institute, and Director of the Fishery Council.

1. Pour 3 pints of water into bottom section of clam steamer.
2. Place top section on lower section and cover bottom of top section with about 2 dozen large hard clams. These are for juice and not to be eaten.
3. On top of them place a layer of wet seaweed. Use plenty of it.
4. On top of this another layer of large clams.
5. Now:

Wrap each vegetable in a square of cheesecloth and tie it so the serving may be easily removed.

> (Wrap 8 medium-sized potatoes, unpeeled
> 8 medium-sized onions, unpeeled
> 4 ears of corn, husks intact, silks removed)

Wrap 1 dozen small clams in a square of cheesecloth, and tie them up. Make 4 of these bundles, using 4 dozen clams.

Place vegetables and small clams on top of layer of large clams.

6. Place 2 salmon steaks on narrow shingle. Tie cheese-cloth around them. This keeps salmon from falling to pieces. Place on top of vegetables and small clams.
7. On top of all this settle two live lobsters. Add 2 or 3 celery stalks and a handful of seaweed.
8. Right in center, on top, put one medium-sized potato. This is your thermometer. When this potato is done, the feast has steamed enough. It takes approximately 1½ hours.

HOW TO SERVE

Fill cups with clam juice; add lemon juice and butter. Clams are to be removed from shells and dipped in melted butter as eaten. Add a little lime or lemon to the salmon. Put lots of melted butter on the lobster, as well as the wonderful corn. Salt, pepper, and butter on potatoes and onions.

How-to-do a Fast Lunch for a Busy Day

1. Mix together 1 can beef soup and 1 can tomato soup, adding water as directed on cans.
2. Stir in a chunk of butter, or chicken fat, and simmer.
3. Add a few thin slices of celery and strew minced parsley on top just as it's ready to serve. Eat with brown bread and butter and hot tea. What is left may be served in cups for supper.

HOW-TO-DO
A PINEAPPLE SURPRISE SUPPER

This is a grand week-end menu solution as the servings may be made up at any time, wrapped individually in waxed paper, and kept in the refrigerator ready to bake at the ring of your doorbell!

Assemble these ingredients on a tray:

1 can sliced pineapple (8 to 10 slices)
1 pound ground smoked ham, mixed with
    1 beaten egg
3 cups mashed yams (or sweet potatoes), mixed with
    2 tablespoons butter
    ½ teaspoon cinnamon

½ teaspoon ginger
2 tablespoons brown sugar or honey
Dash of salt
Drop or 2 of tabasco
2 tablespoons broken pecans
16 strips thin bacon

1. Beat the egg slightly and stir it into the ground ham. Lay 5 circles of pineapple in a shallow baking dish, well buttered.

2. Form the yam mixture into thick patties the same size as the pineapple.

3. Roll the yam patties in finely powdered crumbs and place them on top of the pineapple circles.

4. Next, form the ham into patties of the same size and place them on top of the yam patties.

5. Then top 'em all with another circle of pineapple.

6. Last, crisscross 2 strips of bacon over each stack and fasten the ends of the bacon on the bottom with a toothpick.

7. Bake in a 375-degree oven for 20 minutes if the ham is precooked; in a 350-degree oven for 45 minutes if uncooked ham is used. Buy ham from shank end, removing any gristle. Sometimes in an emergency I have used

ground boiled ham and even canned sweet potatoes.
A substitute of course, but good anyhow.

Serves 8.

HOW-TO-DO
MERCEDES' CHILE CON QUESO

Chile con queso served with a crisp tossed salad, an iced
drink, and tortillas makes a good, easy, and different
luncheon menu.

For a real Mexican dinner, serve *chile con queso* with
tamale pie (page 96), *guacamole* (page 262), and fresh
pineapple for dessert.

Chile con queso means cheese with chile powder.

Tortillas are available in all good Mexican restaurants.
In most places they may be bought in cans.

You will need:

2 medium-sized onions	3 cans tomato paste (1 No.
1 clove garlic	2½ can tomatoes may be
1 red pepper	used instead of tomato
½ cube butter	paste)
2 tablespoons chile powder	1 lb. American cheese
Salt	2 eggs, well beaten

1. Peel onions and garlic and put them with the red pepper through the meat grinder, or chop fine.

2. Melt butter in a large heavy skillet.

3. Put ground onions, garlic, and red pepper in melted
   butter and cook until the onions are soft and yellow,
   but NOT brown.

4. Add chile powder and salt.

5. Add tomato paste, or canned tomatoes. If tomato paste is used it will be necessary to cook the mixture only long enough to blend the onions and tomato paste thoroughly. If canned tomatoes are used, it will take a little longer. Cook until the tomatoes are mushy and some of the juice has cooked away. About 10 minutes.

6. Add cheese, cut into small pieces. (I put mine through the meat grinder when I grind the onions, etc.) Cook over low heat until cheese is melted.

7. Turn out the fire and add the eggs, well beaten, stirring them into the tomato mixture.

Serve on crisp crackers, or melba toast.

Serves 6.

HOW-TO-DO MACARONI AND CHEESE

You will need:

1 eight-oz. package macaroni	1/4 teaspoon salt
1/2 pound of Cheddar cheese	1/2 teaspoon dry mustard
2 eggs	Black pepper
3 cups milk	

1. Cook 8-ounce package of macaroni in 8 cups of rapidly boiling salted water for 10 minutes (1 teaspoon salt).

2. Grate Cheddar cheese.

3. Beat eggs until light and foamy and add salt, dry mustard, and plenty of freshly ground black pepper. Stir in milk.

4. Butter a 2-quart casserole. Pour drained macaroni in. Add cheese and mix well.

5. Now add the milk and egg mixture and dot generously on top with butter.

6. Bake in 400-degree oven 30 minutes.

Serves 4 generously.

This is a satisfying supper serving and one my family recommends as tops. We like carrot strips, cucumber stalks, and celery to go with it. Baked apples seem so right for dessert and iced coffee is good, even in cold weather, for a finale.

How-to-do
a Sturdy Sandwich for House Cleaning Day

1. Spread slice of whole-wheat bread with cream cheese whipped fluffy with plain cream or with sour cream.

2. On top of this spread dried apricots, simmered and drained of their juice.

3. Top with a thin slice of broiled Canadian bacon, or with crisply broiled plain bacon.

4. Cover with a second slice of whole-wheat bread spread with the cheese mixture.

A celery stalk or two is good accompaniment and a glass of buttermilk helps.

There's lots of good fuel to finish the day with and you'll not be cross at the close of a tough day.

NOTE: This is a mighty good sandwich to send along for a school lunch, an office lunch, or even for a hike.

HOW-TO-DO
LELAND'S YACHT CLUB BEANS

This recipe was unearthed by my husky big brother, who has no yacht yet, but who does have a wonderful barbecue shack and serves these beans by the gallon. Sounds like a lot of ingredients, but it's really no trouble.

You will need:

3 cups navy beans
½ cup stuffed green olives

½ cup sweet mixed pickles
2 slices pineapple

Make a sauce using

½ cup olive oil
1 large can tomatoes (No. 2)
1 clove garlic
½ teaspoon salt

½ teaspoon black pepper
½ teaspoon tabasco
3 tablespoons brown sugar
3 tablespoons molasses

1 small bunch celery (½ doz. inner stalks)

Simply place olive oil, mashed tomatoes, garlic, salt, pepper, tabasco, brown sugar, molasses, and finely sliced celery in a saucepan and simmer for at least 30 minutes, stirring frequently. It should be richly thickened. Remove garlic when done. I always stick a toothpick into the clove of garlic, then it's easy to find.

1. Pick over and wash beans and soak them overnight.

2. Cover well with water. Add 1 teaspoon salt and cook at simmering heat for about 3 hours, or until nearly done, but never soft or mushy.

3. Drain and add the sauce, stirring through the beans.

4. Now add stuffed olives, thinly sliced, and the pickles cut in small chunks. (I always buy sweet pickles which

have several little white onions in the jar, for the onions add a lot.) Add the pineapple, cut into small cubes.

5. Turn all into a deep casserole, or a beanpot, and bake for 1 hour. Be sure there is plenty of sauce, as they must not be dry. If necessary, add a small amount hot water to keep them very moist.

Serves 8.

HOW-TO-DO SHISH KEBAB

If you have a barbecue kettle or a grill, then you'll want to buy several of those long heavy skewers to broil and serve *shish kebab* correctly. Wonderful for week-end guests.

You will need:

Leg of lamb	1 tablespoon salt
½ lb. sweet onions	1 teaspoon oregano
½ cup olive oil	Tabasco sauce
½ cup sherry wine	Pepper

Buy a leg of young lamb and ask your market man to cut it into cubes about 1½ inches across. He will first bone it and remove all the fat and gristle.

1. Place meat in your largest mixing bowl.

2. Slice sweet onions paper-thin and mix them through the meat.

3. In a small bowl, mix olive oil with sherry wine and stir in salt, oregano, a few drops of tabasco, and plenty of freshly ground black pepper. Stir well and pour over lamb cubes in bowl. Keep covered in refriger-

ator overnight. Stir meat and sauce together several times.

4. When ready to serve, run skewer through center of each cube. Don't press pieces too close together.

5. Drain on soft paper and broil over charcoal or in your broiler until brown and crusty on the outside and pink and juicy on the inside.

6. Serve immediately . . . HOT.

Serves 12 to 15.

How-to-do a Favorite Sunday-night Supper

Many years ago I had luncheon with Marye Dahnke in her sunny yellow dining room in the Kraft Cheese plant in Chicago. She is truly a culinary artist who loves her work, which is making food interesting and beautiful. She stars cheese, of course, but because she knows food, her menus and recipes are refreshingly stimulating.

The luncheon served to me was never forgotten and I consider it absolutely perfect. So I promptly mastered the recipes and adopted this menu for my own, and I serve it for Sunday-night supper instead of for luncheon. I'd love to share it with you.

MARYE DAHNKE'S CHEESE SOUFFLÉ LUNCHEON

Honeydew Melon with Lime Wedge
Cheese Soufflé
with
Crisp Broiled Bacon
Hot French Bread
Green Salad with French Dressing
Any Favorite Fruit Dessert
Tea

Place the hot casserole on a big blue chop plate, which complements the soft yellow cheese soufflé. Arrange crisply broiled slices of bacon on the chop plate around the casserole. Eat bacon with your fingers, because it's well drained and crisp.

I am partial to my poached fruit for dessert at my Sunday-night suppers (page 223).

HOW-TO-DO CHEESE SOUFFLÉ

You will need:

4 tablespoons butter or margarine	1 teaspoon salt
4 tablespoons flour	Dash cayenne
1½ cups milk	½ lb. process Cheddar cheese, sliced

6 eggs

1. Make a white sauce of the first 5 ingredients.
2. When it is thickened and smooth, add ½ pound sliced process Cheddar cheese. Stir until cheese melts.
3. Remove from the heat and slowly add 6 beaten egg yolks, while stirring constantly. Cool the mixture slightly.
4. In a large mixing bowl, beat the 6 egg whites until very stiff, but not dry.
5. Now slowly fold the cheese sauce into the beaten egg whites. Pour sauce on top of the whites, a small amount at a time. Fold and mix together thoroughly, but gently. Remember that you want to keep all the air bubbles from being broken, so make each folding motion do its best. Each time try to mix the sauce into the whites with fewer strokes.

6. Carefully pour this light mixture into a 2-quart casserole. Don't break bubbles down getting mixture into casserole.

7. With a teaspoon, draw a line around the casserole 1 inch in from the edge. This forms a crease which, when baked, makes a brown crusty "top hat."

8. Bake 1¼ hours in slow oven, 300 degrees.

9. Serve immediately.

You will be sure of success, if you follow these A-B-C's:

a. Use a smooth melting cheese with a sharp Cheddar flavor.

b. Use a 2-quart casserole, not more or less than 2½ inches deep.

c. Use a slow oven, not more than 300 degrees, and remember this soufflé is worth waiting for, so do not make it wait for the family. Serve immediately.

How-to-do "Oh My Heavens" Dishes
(For Little Meals)

Every homemaker has had the experience of unexpected guests when the menu will not stretch. Here are some of my old tested answers. We call them "Oh My Heavens" dishes because the family declares that I invariably come back from the phone and say "Oh my heavens—Mr. and Mrs. McGillucity are on the way over—quick, you start grating this half pound cheese and I'll make an omelet."

So there is an omelet in my Oh My Heavens file. There is a sea-food shortcake (you'll find the recipe on page 239). Special guests on the Oh My Heavens list may be offered Mercedes' Chile con Queso.

For an emergency dessert, try Floating Island.

I keep the dough for all bran rolls (page 98) in the refrigerator and these hot rolls are wonderful for Oh My Heavens menu material.

My Special Clam Soup is a sudden serving which always makes an impression.

When I whisk out a meringue dessert, guests always feel that I've spent the day getting ready for them. Actually it requires all of six minutes to whip vanilla ice cream till slightly fluffy—not melted—and add any kind of sliced or chopped fruit. Ladle this into attractive dessert dishes and settle a meringue (page 177) in the center. Top with a cherry or more fruit. Serve.

EMERGENCY SUPPLIES TO THE RESCUE

I keep a cupboard well stocked with my favorite cans of fruit. Another one of the easiest Oh My Heavens menus is fruit salad with Cardinal Dressing (page 76), a platter of grilled Canadian bacon, and frizzled dried beef with hot all bran rolls and sweet butter.

My soups are lifesavers and I consider all of them worth a spot on Oh My Heavens menus.

Hot breads save the day, also waffles. Driving in from a week end with guests, I'll hear myself saying "Come on in for waffles—we always have them on Sunday night."

By the time guests argue a few minutes and accept, I've mentally checked my shelf—"Plenty of eggs, milk, butter, maple sirup, and, happily, a fruit dessert—guess I didn't speak too quickly."

If you'll keep a jar of hollandaise sauce in your refrigerator and a can of processed ham and a box of rusks on your shelf, an impromptu serving of Eggs Benedict really pleases and impresses guests and solves the problem of another Oh My Heavens menu.

If I could make just one wish for your menu solutions, so you'd really find the pot of gold at the foot of your kitchen rainbow, I'd wish for every homemaker to have and to use a big home freeze.

OUR OH MY HEAVENS OMELET

1. In a large mixing bowl, beat 4 egg yolks until thick and pale lemon-colored.

2. Add salt and plenty of freshly ground black pepper.

3. Now melt ½ pound freshly grated cheese over hot water, stirring well, and add 4 tablespoons top milk or cream, stirring until nice and smooth. Do not let water boil.

4. Remove from heat and cool a minute.

5. Pour cheese mixture into egg yolks just a little at a time and beat thoroughly.

6. Next, beat the egg whites till stiff, but not dry.

7. Then fold the egg whites into the cheese mix-

ture, cutting and folding the air bubbles (page 291) gently.

8. Heat 4 tablespoons butter in a large, heavy skillet. It should be foamy hot, but NOT browned.

9. Pour omelet mixture into skillet and keep heat low. It must cook slowly until set and puffed up to the top of the skillet. Do NOT cook too fast.

10. Now place skillet in a very slow oven, about 300 degrees, to dry omelet on top. Requires only 3 or 4 minutes.

11. Remove from oven and using long spatula fold one half of omelet over on top of the other half.

Serves 4.

I find this folding more easily done if I cut a short gash at each side of the omelet, making a kind of hinge. Slip it out of the skillet onto a heated chop plate and garnish with crisp watercress.

Vary by spreading half of the omelet, before folding, with sautéed mushrooms, or ripe tomatoes thinly sliced, or creole sauce, or tart plum jam, or leftover vegetables.

Must be served pronto.

SOUPS FOR THE LITTLE MEAL

HOW-TO-DO CREAM OF CORN SOUP

This is one of my favorite soup servings. You may as well copy the recipe onto cards and slip them into the buffet drawer when you serve it, as guests always ask for it.

You will need:

4 tablespoons butter	1 teaspoon beef extract
3 tablespoons flour	1 teaspoon onion juice
½ teaspoon salt	or grated onion
Plenty of freshly ground	3 cups milk
black pepper	1 can cream-style corn *or*

Equal amount green corn *

1. In heavy saucepan, melt butter and stir in flour, cooking over LOW heat and stirring carefully until a smooth paste is made. (It should taste well done, not raw or floury.)

2. Add all seasonings and slowly stir in milk. Keep heat low until mixture is smooth. Add corn, increase heat, and let soup come to boiling point. Don't let it boil though.

3. Quickly turn heat down and simmer for 15 minutes.

4. Add a chunk of butter and more freshly ground black pepper.

5. Serve piping hot in heated bowls.

We like hot crusty toasted buns with this soup. I split the buns and toast them under the broiler. Then turn them, brush generously with butter, and sprinkle with sesame seed. Then toast other side golden brown. Serve HOT.

* If you use green corn, be sure to select young, tender ears of corn. Cut off thin slices of corn from the cob and then, using the back of your knife, scrape all milk and pulp from the cob.

When you run canned corn (cream style) through food mill be sure to throw away all outside dry portion which will not go through the mill. I sometimes dash a very little hot water over these dry husks and save a little of the goodness.

HOW-TO-DO ONION SOUP

4 big yellow onions sliced
   paper-thin
4 tablespoons butter
4 cups hot water

5 beef-bouillon cubes
Black pepper and salt
Dash tabasco sauce
½ cup red wine

1. Slice onions paper-thin and don't use hard end.

2. In a large skillet, heat butter till it bubbles, but does not brown.

3. Add onions. Keep heat moderately low. Using wide spatula turner, gently turn onions to cook evenly.

4. Keep heat low and don't mash onions turning them. Do not scorch, or you'll have a bitter bad taste. Be sure to remove any portion which accidentally scorches.

5. Add salt, pepper, and 4 cups of bouillon (made by adding the 5 beef-bouillon cubes to the 4 cups of hot water and stirring to dissolve).

6. Turn heat high and bring to boil.

7. Watch carefully till boiling starts, then cut heat down to low simmer. Cover and simmer ½ hour, or until onions are perfectly tender. When done, add ½ cup red wine.

8. As onion soup simmers, heat your best earthenware casserole and toast and butter 4 slices of French bread.

9. When onions are very tender, turn soup into heated casserole and drop the toasted French bread on top to float.

10. Sprinkle about 2 tablespoons freshly grated Parmesan cheese on each slice and place in very hot oven, 425 degrees, to brown the cheese and glaze the soup serving on top.

11. Ladle into heated bowls, serving generous portions of onions in each bowl and floating the toast. Pass hot French bread also and complete this fare with a green salad and fruit and iced coffee.

HOW-TO-DO DOUBLE QUICK SOUP

For a hot serving when it's sandwich or salad night, a really good soup extends the menu and puts the family or guests in a satisfied easy-to-serve mood.

You will need:

1 box dehydrated pea soup	Black pepper
4 cups hot milk	Minced chives
4 tablespoons butter	1 pound fresh crab
Paprika	

1. Pour a package of dried pea soup into 4 cups of hot milk and cook as directed on package.

2. Add 2 tablespoons of butter, freshly ground black pepper, and a few snips of minced chives.

3. Remove thin bony pieces from ½ pound fresh crab and sauté it in 2 tablespoons of sweet butter.

4. Ladle soup into heated bowls and add a generous portion of crab to each bowl.

5. Dust on top with paprika.

6. Serve hot with toasted whole-wheat rolls buttered.

Serves 6 to 8.

HOW-TO-DO STREAMLINED BEAN SOUP

One day I promised my best bean soup to the family, but due to circumstances beyond my control (as they say in television) I didn't get it made. Instead, I stirred up a quick version which has become a request number ever since.

You will need:

2 cans baked beans	2 tablespoons butter
4 cups water	1 tablespoon flour
1 medium onion	¼ cup milk
2 stalks celery with leaves	Tabasco sauce, Worcester-
1 cup tomato catsup	shire, pepper
End of ham	

1. Turn the cans of beans into a large kettle.

2. Add water, onion, celery with leaves, tomato catsup, and an end piece of ham with or without bone.

3. Put that tight lid on and simmer for 30 minutes. Remove ham and then strain through food mill (or ricer if no food mill). Add salt to taste.

4. Make a paste of butter and flour with the milk. Add to soup, stirring and cooking until slightly thickened, with no raw taste (about 10 minutes).

5. Add several dashes of tabasco sauce, Worcestershire, and freshly ground black pepper.

6. Serve in sturdy bowls very hot. Drop in a few bites of the ham if you like.

Serves 6.

MAIN DISHES FOR THE LITTLE MEAL

HOW-TO-DO STEAK STICKS

Buy 1 pound of beef round, about ¾ inch thick and 1 pound of veal round, about ¾ inch thick. Ask your market man for 8 wooden skewers.

You will also need:

1 cup fine crumbs	2 tablespoons shortening
1 egg	2 tablespoons butter

1. Cut meat into even chunks nearly 1 inch square.
2. Now run a chunk of beef onto a skewer, then a chunk of veal. Continue until the skewer is full of the squares of meat. Do not press close together.
3. Next, dip the stick of meat into slightly-beaten egg mixed with 1 tablespoon water.
4. Then roll it in a mound of finely powdered bread crumbs.
5. In a heavy skillet, heat 2 tablespoons of butter with 2 tablespoons of shortening. Skillet should be very hot, but should not scorch the butter.
6. Brown the meat sticks quickly until crusty brown all over. Turn them. Dust with salt and black pepper.
7. When all are golden brown, place a good tight lid on the skillet and turn the heat down low.
8. Cook gently about 45 minutes, or until the meat is so tender and moist you can cut it with a fork.

NOTE: Important to brown meat quickly, cover skillet tightly, finish cooking slowly. Test to be sure meat is tender and juicy.

Serve on bed of fluffy white rice (page 149) and make cream gravy with leavings in skillet (page 114).

HOW-TO-DO HARRYETTE'S CHEESE GOO

You will need:

1 pound processed cheese, diced	1 four-oz. can chili peppers, drained and diced
2 tablespoons condensed milk	1 teaspoon garlic salt
1 cup canned tomato pulp (well drained)	½ teaspoon paprika

¼ teaspoon each salt, onion salt, celery salt

1. Melt cheese with milk in heavy skillet (or in double boiler), stirring carefully over low heat.
2. When smooth, add tomato pulp, peppers, and all seasonings. Mix well.
3. Store in jars and keep in refrigerator.
4. Serve on potato chips or on crackers.

Makes about 1 pint.

This spread keeps indefinitely and is delicious. Nice to serve to teleguests, and easy on the grocery budget.

How-to-do Baked Red Kidney Beans

This is a serving good for a quick supper and it is economical as well as easy to do. Serve with buttered cauliflower, hot garlic bread, baked apples, and black coffee or buttermilk.

1. To 1 can red kidney beans, add 1 small onion and 1 pickle, minced, or use ¼ cup pickle relish.
2. Mince 2 stalks of celery and add.

3. Next, stir in 1 teaspoon dry mustard and 4 tablespoons sour cream.

4. Turn into baking dish and bake in 350-degree oven for 25 minutes.

Lickin' good to eat!

HOW-TO-DO ZELLA AND BOB'S SUPPER

Good when all the grandchildren come in for supper.

You will need, to start:

1 large onion	5 tablespoons butter
1 green pepper	2 pounds ground steak

1. Cook sliced onion and pepper in the butter, stirring constantly over medium heat for 10 minutes.

2. Add the ground steak and brown lightly.

3. Simmer in a saucepan for 10 minutes:

1 No. 2 can of tomatoes	3 teaspoons salt
1 teaspoon sugar	¼ teaspoon soda

4. Boil 1 package of broken spaghetti 5 minutes and drain.

5. Stir mixtures together.

6. Add 1 teaspoon chili powder, dash of red pepper, one cup cream, ½ cup milk, ¼ pound of American cheese, grated.

7. Mix all together and pour into large buttered casserole.

8. Cover with tight lid.

9. Bake in 375-degree oven 2 hours.

Serves 6 to 8.

How-to-do Volcano Potatoes—a Surprise

Trying to vary our menus not only brings in new and untried foods, but stimulates us to try new tricks with old, regular foods. For example, mashed potatoes really perk up the menu when prepared this way. A mighty good substitute for meat, too. May be prepared early in the day and reheated for dinner, but if you do this be sure to use plenty of milk in the mashed potatoes and then heat them thoroughly so they'll be puffy and moist.

1. Cook 4 large potatoes and mash as usual.
2. Pour the mashed potatoes into a well-buttered baking dish. (I like to use a Pyrex pie dish.)
3. Pile them high to make a cone-shaped volcano.
4. Now dig a well down into the center, large enough to hold about a cup and one half of the rich cheese sauce.
5. Pour the cheese sauce into the well and top with the potato you dug out.
6. Brush with melted butter and dust with fine, sifted bread crumbs.
7. Place in hot oven to heat through and to brown lightly.

Mighty good eating!

HOW-TO-DO CHEESE SAUCE

2 tablespoons butter
2 tablespoons flour
¼ teaspoon each salt and paprika

Freshly ground black pepper
1 cup milk
½ pound grated cheese

1. Melt butter and blend in flour and seasonings, stirring over low heat.

2. Add milk and stir constantly to make thick smooth sauce.

3. Add grated cheese and stir over low heat only until cheese melts.

Serves 4 to 6.

How-to-do Egg Cutlets

This is an unusual substitute for meat and it is economical, easy to prepare, and delicious to eat.

Egg cutlets may be prepared early in the day—formed into shapes, dipped in egg and crumbs, and placed in the refrigerator until ready to fry. If you keep them cold, be sure to set them out so they will become room temperature before frying. Sometimes I make my best mushroom sauce and serve over them.

1. In heavy saucepan, melt 4 tablespoons of butter and add 4 tablespoons flour.

2. Stir over low heat until a smooth paste is made.

3. Add 2 cups of milk. Increase heat and stir until thickened and smooth.

4. Add ¼ teaspoon of salt and plenty of black pepper, 1 teaspoon onion juice or grated onion, and a few drops of tabasco sauce.

5. Stir in 1 tablespoon finely minced parsley and 6 hardcooked eggs which have been chopped into good-sized squares, not too fine.

6. Turn mixture out onto plate and chill in refrigerator.

7. When perfectly cold, dip out a large tablespoonful and form into cutlet shape.

8. Dip in fine bread crumbs (I use grated rusks), then in slightly beaten eggs, again into a mound of fine crumbs.

9. Fry in deep hot fat, 375 degrees, until golden brown.

10. Drain on soft paper and serve from heated platter garnished with parsley and lemon wedges.

Serves 6 to 8.

NOTE: 1 cup diced chicken may be added to the mixture, which of course adds more food value. If you do not want to use the deep-fat kettle, just fry the cutlets in a heavy skillet with sufficient fat to prevent burning. Turn just once!

HOW-TO-DO MEAT PIE

This meat pie is designed to use up leftovers in the refrigerator. Exact amounts are not required, but the following is a basic to use and to vary as you like. Serve with a flourish, not mentioning leftovers, and expect applause.

You will need:

1 to 2 cups meat	4 carrots, cooked, cut into
1 cup stock or gravy	big slices
Salt and pepper to taste	1 large sweet onion, cubed
½ bay leaf	2 stalks celery, thickly sliced
Pinch of marjoram	1 cup cooked peas
1 large cooked potato, cut	Corn or tomatoes (optional)
into chunks	

Leftover meat and gravy from roast may be used, or any other leftover meat. If none, buy ½ pound beef, chuck or some other less expensive cut, and ½ pound pork.

1. Cut meat into good-sized bites.
2. Roll in flour and brown quickly in 4 tablespoons hot fat, turning carefully.
3. Add 1 cup of stock and all seasonings.
4. Adjust a good tight lid and *simmer* about 45 minutes, or until tender.
5. Add all vegetables, which have been cooked about done and seasoned.
6. Turn into baking dish or pan having plenty of surface.
7. Top with Pin-wheel Biscuits (page 135).
8. Bake in 450-degree oven for 25 minutes, or until biscuits are cooked through and browned.

Serves 4 to 6.

How-to-do Emergency Tuna Shortcake

Measurements are not exact in this recipe. Maybe you'll want to use more or less tuna. You might decide to add a cup of leftover peas or green corn or vary the seasonings, or add a bit of sherry. It's your emergency offering. Go to it.

1. Begin by *keeping* on your emergency shelf 2 or 3 cans of tuna fish, canned mushroom soup, biscuit mix, olives, and pimientos.
2. Stir up shortcake dough and bake as for strawberry shortcake (page 170).
3. Pour 1 can of mushroom soup into saucepan and add ½ cup cream, 2 tablespoons butter, about 1 tablespoon chives, a few drops of tabasco sauce, and a dash of Accent.

4. Cook over *low* heat, stirring well, for about 5 minutes.

5. Add 1 or 2 cans tuna broken into large chunks, not minced. Carefully heat it in the sauce. Add 1 or 2 pimientos and several ripe olives cut in slices and heat 2 or 3 minutes more. Keep hot over hot water.

6. Lift top layer of shortcake to large chop plate and turn crust side down.

7. Pour tuna and sauce over this hot shortcake, covering it generously.

8. Settle other layer over it, crust side up, and pour remaining hot sauce and tuna on top.

9. Be sure to strew sliced ripe olives and pimiento strips over top.

10. Serve piping hot.

Serves 4 to 6.

How-to-do Simmered Chicken

For chicken salad, chow mein, Chicken Velvet Soup, club sandwiches, chicken à la king, and chicken and dumplings I've insisted in these recipes that you simmer, not *boil,* a good fat hen or fowl. It is important.

Buy a good fat hen or fowl weighing at least 4 or 5 pounds. Ask for the feet, as there's so much gelatin quality in them which is fine in the broth. Leave the chicken whole, so all the quality from the bones is retained. Also you'll get nicer slices.

1. Clean chicken carefully, removing all organs along backbone, and rinse under the cold-water faucet.

Don't let this offend you—But there's nothing like taking a good honest whiff of any chicken to be sure it's thoroughly cleaned. I'd much rather test it while cleaning than while eating.

2. Place fowl in a *deep* kettle with that good old *tight lid.* Add about 8 cups of warm (not boiling) water and a soup bouquet—a stalk of celery with all its leaves, a carrot, half a medium onion, 2 or 3 sprigs of parsley, and 3 or 4 peppercorns.

3. Turn the heat up to bring it to the boiling point quickly. Watch. Don't let boiling continue, as it draws the juices out and toughens chicken. Next, turn heat down to a low simmer. Put that tight lid on and let it simmer for about 2½ to 3 hours, or until chicken is perfectly tender. Add 1 teaspoon salt about the last 15 minutes.

4. Let chicken cool in the stock, as it will absorb moisture and be juicy, flavorful, and delicious.

HOW-TO-DO CHICKEN PAPRIKA

This is one of our favorite Sunday-night supper servings. I prepare it on Saturday, leave it in the refrigerator until 1 hour before serving, then turn it into my Mexican pottery baking dish and finish as given in Steps 5 through 7.

You will need:

One 2½ to 3-pound fryer	2 cups chicken stock
Flour	2 tablespoons paprika
Approximately ½ cup shortening and butter, mixed half and half	Garlic or chives
	Salt and black pepper
	1 cup sour cream

1. Prepare chicken and brown exactly as for frying. Be sure to save the neck and bony back pieces out to make 2 cups of stock (page 136).

2. When chicken is carefully browned, add 1½ cups stock and 2 tablespoons of good Hungarian paprika. Shake it all over the chicken, turning several times. It is practically red with paprika, but oh how good!

3. Sometimes I stick a toothpick into a clove of garlic and drop it into the skillet with the chicken. Remove it later. (That's why the toothpick—so it's easily located.) Sometimes I add 2 tablespoons of chives as it goes into the casserole.

4. Now put that good tight lid on and turn heat LOW. Simmer covered for 1 hour (2½ to 3-pound chicken). Turn two or three times.

5. Remove chicken to baking dish.

6. Scrape all crusty particles from skillet and stir in 1 cup fresh sour cream. Mix well and keep heat really low. Don't boil that cream!

7. Pour all this good sauce over chicken and place baking dish in 325-degree oven just long enough to heat thoroughly.

Serves 4.

How-to-do Real Potato Salad

1. Add salt, a slice of onion, and a few peppercorns to the water in which potatoes are cooked.

2. Cook 5 medium-sized potatoes (2½ pounds) in their jackets until tender, but not overdone.

3. When potatoes are tender, drain and shake dry over high heat.

4. Skin them and while still hot cut into nice bite-sized pieces. Sprinkle lightly with salt and freshly ground black pepper.

5. Now to the steaming hot potatoes add 4 tablespoons of marinade, made by combining olive oil and vinegar in equal portions (2 tablespoons oil and 2 tablespoons wine vinegar).

6. Splash this over the potatoes and mix by turning the potatoes from one bowl to another so they will not be broken or mushy.

7. Place in refrigerator to chill.

8. When cold, add 3 sliced hard-cooked eggs; 2 or 3 new green onions, tops and all, diced; 2 inner stalks of celery, cut in slices; 1 cucumber, cut into chunks, and 2 teaspoons of capers. Be sure to leave some of the skin on the cucumber and salt it lightly.

9. When ready to serve, mix lightly with from 1/3 to ½ cup mayonnaise.

10. Pile on chilled glass chop plate and surround with crisp lettuce cups. Sprinkle crisp parsley on top and serve with fanfare.

Serves 6.

How-to-do Exciting Chicken Salad

Of course there is chicken salad—and—chicken salad! The hashed-together kind covered up with mayonnaise is no kin to the one I offer here. First, the chicken must be gently simmered in well-seasoned broth until perfectly tender (page 240). Next, let it cool in the broth. Now lift the chicken out and remove every bit of skin, then cut the meat into nice big bites.

1. In a deep bowl, place 2½ to 3 cups chicken cut into generous bites.

2. Add 1 cup chopped celery, using tender inside stalks. Don't chop too fine. (I like Pascal celery when available.)

3. Cut 1 hard-cooked egg into cubes and season with salt and freshly ground black pepper. Add to bowl.

4. Slice 10 or 12 ripe olives in strips and add.

5. Sprinkle in ¼ teaspoon of celery seed and ¼ teaspoon white mustard seed. Taste for salt and black pepper.

6. Sprinkle about 2 tablespoons lemon or lime juice over chicken mixture and stir lightly.

7. Add 1/3 cup mayonnaise and toss lightly together.

8. Let stand in refrigerator to blend and "ripen" and serve in crisp lettuce cups.

9. Just before serving add ¼ cup blanched almonds cut in two.

For variation I often add ½ cup chilled pineapple chunks, well drained. And on scorching hot days 1 cupful of chilled Thompson seedless grapes add immensely to the coolness and quality of this salad. In wintertime add canned white cherries, seeds removed, or peel and seed big Tokay grapes.

Serves 6 to 8.

HOW-TO-DO GOOD OLD BEAN SALAD

You will need:

2 cups red beans
1 cup celery, chopped
2 tablespoons minced onion
1/8 teaspoon salt
2 tablespoons green pepper, diced

2 pimientos, sliced
2 hard-cooked eggs
1 cup raw apple, unpeeled and chopped
1/2 cup cheese, diced
1/2 cup salad dressing

1. Just drain the large red kidney beans and add other ingredients in the order listed.

2. Set in refrigerator to chill.

3. Drain well and serve in big lettuce cups.

Serves 4 to 6.

How-to-do Persimmon Salad Superb

You may not have been concerned over the fact that these huge golden persimmons are on our markets only a limited few weeks. But when you've served this superb salad once, you will watch for them eagerly, ever after.

Buy large ripe persimmons when they are really ripe.

1. Place persimmons bud end down on salad plates.

2. Using a sharp paring knife, cut from the smaller end toward the bud end, making four sections or petals. Pull them apart.

3. Form a ball of cottage cheese lightly mixed with a little sour cream and a dash of salt.

4. Drop this into the center of each persimmon and pass

French dressing made with lemon. My Cardinal Dressing (page 76) is also perfect with this salad.

One persimmon to each.

* * *

HOW-TO-DO COTTAGE CHEESE TARTLETS

Serve these flaky bites piping hot for a lift to your party. The dough may be made, rolled in waxed paper, and kept for days. An hour or so before time to serve, set the dough out to become room temperature. Then roll thinly and make into tartlets. Bake at the last moment and serve to the tune of delight from your family and your guests. P.S. Make plenty.

You will need:

½ cup butter or margarine
½ cup cottage cheese, well drained

1 cup all-purpose flour
Strawberry preserves

1. Cream butter and cottage cheese until light and fluffy.
2. Work and stir in flour and blend until smooth ball of dough is formed.
3. Chill 30 minutes.
4. Then roll thin.
5. Cut into 3-inch squares.
6. Drop a scant teaspoon of strawberry preserves into center of each square and turn dough over preserves to form a triangle.
7. Press edges tight together with tines of a fork.
8. Place on ungreased baking sheet, not touching.

9. Bake in hot oven, 425 degrees, for from 12 to 15 minutes. Remove from baking sheet while hot and cool on wire cake rack.

Makes 2 dozen 3-inch tartlets.

DESSERTS FOR THE LITTLE MEAL

How-to-do Dessert Surprises

1. Did you ever buy molds of vanilla ice cream and pour chocolate sirup over them, then dust them with Saigon cinnamon?

2. Did you ever make a shortcake by placing 1 rusk in a dessert bowl, topping it with baked rhubarb and placing a second hot buttered rusk on that? Then serve with sour cream, icy cold?

HOW-TO-DO
NETTIE'S GREENGAGE SHERBET

You will need:

1 can greengage plums with all the juice	¼ cup confectioners' sugar
2 tablespoons lime juice with grated rind	½ cup white corn sirup
	Dash of salt
	1 cup whipping cream

1. Remove seeds from plums and mash well with a fork.

2. Add sugar and stir till dissolved.

3. Pour the corn sirup and the lime juice into the fruit, pouring in a very fine stream and beating constantly with rotary beater.

4. Now pour heavy cream (don't whip) slowly into mix-

ture and beat with rotary beater or electric beater until smooth and foamy.

5. Turn into trays and freeze till mushy.

6. Remove and beat hard.

7. Return to trays and freeze.

This is a refreshing dessert for hot days. Add a few drops of green fruit coloring to give added tint of color. Go easy—pale, delicate green.

Serves 6.

HOW-TO-DO PIXIE'S CUP CAKES

Pixie does these cup cakes very well and you should see her results with the coloring project. She goes to the Museum of Modern Art and is daring with paints. Pixie is age four and already knows the definitions for beat, fold, stir, and mix. She also understands the necessity for "a good tight lid" on all her pans. Try this on your small girls and boys.

You will need:

>1 box cup-cake mix
>1 package white-frosting mix

1. Follow directions on box for cup cakes.

2. Follow directions on box for frosting.

3. Pour frosting into three custard cups.

4. Use pink, yellow, and orchid fruit coloring.

5. Mix each cup of frosting to give delicate colors.

6. Spread on cakes.

7. EAT.

HOW-TO-DO ANNE'S SCOTCH SHORTBREAD

You will need:

> 4 cups cake flour
> ½ cup sugar
> 1 cup butter

1. Sift flour and sugar together.

2. Chop butter into sugar and flour with pastry blender or 2 knives.

3. When thoroughly mixed, go after it with your hands. Work it for several minutes or until you can make small mounds of the mixture, which hold together when you press them with your hand.

4. Next pour mixture into an ungreased pan, 7½ x 11 inches and 2 inches deep.

5. Now here's the trick. This will be crumbly and you'll likely vow I've left something out. Wrong. Just begin pressing the mixture down firmly into the pan. Sometimes I use a wooden mallet to press it smoothly all across the top. Be sure to do it firmly.

6. Bake in 375-degree oven for 45 minutes. It does not brown, but is pale biscuit-colored.

7. It MUST be cut as soon as it comes from the oven. I cut it into 20 pieces, 3½ x 1 inches.

These rich, crunchy strips of shortbread are perfect with fragrant hot tea. They are so easy to make and will keep indefinitely.

*   *   *

How-to-do Hot Tea

1. Draw water for tea from cold-water faucet.
2. Heat in open pan, not the teakettle.
3. Scald a large earthenware pot.
4. As soon as water comes to a full, rounding boil, use it. Allow 1 teaspoon tea leaves for each cup of water.
5. Fill pot with the freshly boiling water and cover closely to steep 4 to 5 minutes, no longer.
6. Now strain the tea into a scalded china pot and take it to the tea table, where it is ready to pour.

If serving a large group, have someone in the kitchen to keep up this routine with another earthenware pot, giving fresh tea as needed.

Do not boil tea. Do not make a little pot of very strong, bitter tea and dilute it with hot water (bad!)

How-to-do Iced Tea

Follow same procedure as for hot tea, pouring the freshly made tea over the ice cubes. Nearly everyone uses 2 teaspoons tea to 1 cup of water for iced tea, as the ice dilutes it. But do not make a little pot of very strong, bitter tea and dilute. There is but one way to make real tea.

SIMPLE SUPPER MENUS

Menu I

My Chicken Chow Mein (page 87)
Gherkins, Finochio, Carrot Sticks, Cucumber Sticks
in Ice Bowl
Drifts of Lime and Raspberry Sherbet
Pots of Hot Tea

Menu II

Cream of Corn Soup (page 228)
Fruit Plate with Cottage Cheese
Twisted Hot Rolls
Pascal Celery
Orange Ice Cream or Caramel Custard
Iced Tea with Mint Sprig

Menu III

Hamburgers Burgundy on Toasted Buns
Relish Tray
Fresh Cherry Pudding (page 175)

Menu IV

Beef Stew (page 116)
Pin-wheel Biscuits (page 135)
Spiced Peaches and Hot Coffee

Maybe an extra pan of the hot biscuits and apple butter with more hot coffee.

Menu V

SOUTHWESTERN SPECIAL

Chile con Carne (page 213)
Hot Tamales
Tortillas
Chilled Pineapple Slices or Chunks
Mugs of Black Coffee (page 33)

Simple hot servings which may be added to extend these menus, or to make them heartier, are my unusual macaroni and cheese, page 219; black-eyed peas with bacon, page 154; Unauthorized Spaghetti Supper, page 235.

MENUS FOR BRUNCH OR LUNCH
Menu I
Rum Flavored Broiled Grapefruit
Cheese Soufflé (page 224)
Canadian Bacon
Red Apple Circles (page 173)
Green Salad, French Dressing
Frozen Raspberries and Wafers
Iced Coffee

Menu II
Old Fashioned Bean Soup (page 232)
with Ham Chunks
Big Squares Hot Corn Bread
New Green Onions   Dill Pickles
Baked Apples
Oatmeal Cookies (page 188)
Coffee

Menu III
Pineapple Surprise Supper (page 217)
Romaine Wedges with Plain French Dressing
Poached Fresh Fruit
Iced Tea

SPECIAL SUPPER MENUS
A Southern Supper in June
Fried Chicken (page 131)
Real Cream Gravy (page 132)
Hot Biscuits
Sliced Tomatoes Covered with Crushed Ice
Fresh Green Onions   Icicle Radishes
New Potatoes in Their Jackets with Parsley Butter
More Hot Biscuits and Fresh Strawberry Preserves
Iced Tea with Mint Sprig

Buffet Supper for Company

Baked Ham
Yacht Club Beans (page 221)
Tossed Green Salad
Garlic Buttered French Bread, Toasted
Individual Strawberry Shortcakes (page 170)

5. Snacks

Everyone should learn to do snacks with their left hand, says one of my friends—then they would stay in their proper place in the daily menu. They would be never too important and yet always on hand to make life a little merrier.

So here we are with a bunch of easy-to-do snacks to serve before dinner with cocktails; at cocktail (or tea) parties; around the TV set, or any other time when nibblers are in demand.

These nibblers are of various kinds. There are:

1. Spreads to mix quickly, to serve with toast, crackers, and *hors d'oeuvre* bits—each to spread his own.

2. Tidbits speared on toothpicks—hot or cold.

3. One-bite sandwiches of many varieties.

P.S. See page 148 for broiled shrimp in chili sauce wrapped in bacon, my favorite snack serving.

HOW-TO-DO A SNACK MEN LIKE

You will need:

1 cup Cheddar cheese, grated	2 teaspoons paprika
2 tablespoons anchovy paste	1 teaspoon mustard
1 tablespoon minced onion	2 tablespoons capers
1 tablespoon chives	1 tablespoon caraway seed

Enough ale or beer to soften so it will spread

Makes 1¼ cups of spread.

How-to-do Pecans for Snacks

Mix 1 cup sugar, 1 teaspoon salt, ½ teaspoon each nutmeg and cloves, 2 teaspoons cinnamon, and ¼ cup water. Cook until sirup forms a soft ball when tested in cold water. Add ½ pound pecans. Remove from heat and stir until sugary. Spread on oiled paper or buttered platter. Break apart when cool.

Gertrude's Brazil Nut Chips

Cover shelled Brazil nuts with hot water. Bring to gentle boil and simmer 5 minutes. Drain and slice lengthwise into long thin slices. Spread out on shallow baking tray. Dot generously with butter. Sprinkle with salt. Toast in hot oven, 400 degrees, from 5 to 8 minutes. Make a lot. They disappear.

Swiss Bits

Run a toothpick through a square of sharp Swiss cheese, then a tiny spiced pickled onion, then another square of cheese. Onion on top. Stand on tray.

How-to-do Toasted Cheese Squares for Teleguests

1. Buy a loaf of white bread, UNSLICED.

2. Remove all crusts.

3. Cut through the center into 2 long pieces.

4. Next cut the 2 pieces lengthwise through the center, leaving 4 long pieces.

5. Now cut each of these 4 long sections into large cubes about 1½ inches across.

6. Melt 1 cube butter and add 2 or 3 drops Worcestershire sauce, 1 teaspoon paprika, and 1 cut clove of garlic. I keep this butter mixture warm by pouring it into a sizzling hot Pyrex dish.

7. Now dip each side of the bread cube into the warm butter mixture, or use a brush to "paint" each side thoroughly with the butter.

8. Next, dip this buttery bread square into a mound of finely powdered Parmesan cheese. Be sure each side of the square is well coated.

9. Place squares on a baking sheet. Don't let them touch.

10. Place in a HOT OVEN (450 degrees) to brown for from 8 to 10 minutes. Do NOT put them under the broiler. USE OVEN. Serve piping hot.

Wonderful with drinks or with coffee. For a cocktail party, a tea, or just for a snack. This is one of my favorites.

HOW-TO-DO ANCHOVY WHEELS

You will need:

> Pie dough (page 182)
> 1 tube anchovy paste
> 1 tablespoon mayonnaise

This snack bite is a definite surprise and I invented it many years ago. To be honest, it was a plain accident which saved the day gloriously.

1. Divide pastry dough in 2 parts. Work with one portion and keep the rest in refrigerator.

2. Roll this one portion just as thin as possible. Shape into a rectangle about 5 x 8 inches and cut the edges evenly.

3. Spread mayonnaise thinly over surface of pastry.

4. Next spread anchovy paste over pastry. Do NOT spread too close to edge as paste will push out as you roll the pastry.

5. Now start at the long end and roll jelly-roll style. Roll tightly and seal long edge down close to roll.

6. Wrap in waxed paper and chill well.

7. Cut into thin slices, place on cooky sheet, and bake in hot, 400-degree, oven for about 8 minutes. Serve hot.

Makes about 4 dozen small wheels.

These rolls may be kept indefinitely and sliced to bake quickly.

How-to-do Cocktail Chicken Livers

1. Buy 1 pound chicken livers, fresh or frozen.
2. Drain on soft paper and separate into single portions.
3. Roll lightly in flour to which salt and pepper have been added.
4. Sauté gently in butter. Requires from 4 to 5 minutes.
5. Drain on soft paper.
6. Now thread half a liver onto a skewer, next add a square of half-done broiled bacon, then a pickled onion and another liver half.
7. Broil quickly.
8. Keep hot in the oven and serve with drinks.

You'll find that these livers served with crackers are no more expensive than varied canapés or mixtures for dipping. It's more unusual and it is delicious. Also, it may be prepared the day before, or well in advance of a party, and then reheated.

HOW-TO-DO LIVER LOAF

You will be surprised at the many ways there are to use this delicious mixture. I think it's better than lots of expensive *pâté's* I've eaten and how it helps for menu material on long week ends! Try it once.

You will need:

1 calf, beef, or pork liver	Dash tabasco or cayenne
1 slice onion	1 teaspoon onion juice (or grated onion)
1 stalk celery with leaves	
1 tablespoon Worcestershire sauce	2 tablespoons mayonnaise

1. Cook liver until tender in water to which the onion slice, celery, salt, and pepper have been added.
2. Bring to a boil, then *simmer* gently till tender.
3. Let cool in its liquor. Then drain well and pat dry with soft paper toweling.
4. When cold, run through meat grinder (or use food mill).
5. Using a wooden spoon, rub this to a paste with remaining seasonings and mayonnaise.
6. Form into a roll. Wrap in waxed paper or in aluminum foil. Chill at least half a day.
7. Slice to serve as cold meat, to use for sandwich makings, for *pâté*. And you will discover many of your own uses for it.

Cut into small bites, spear on toothpicks with cocktail onions, and serve with crackers to teleguests.

How-to-do Camembert and Toasted Crackers

Remove wedges of Camembert from the refrigerator, unwrap, and place on plates to become room temperature. The cheese should be runny and never served hard or firm.

Toast crackers lightly and serve with the cheese. A dead ripe pear may be served with the cheese instead of crackers. Black coffee is a must with this dessert serving.

How-to-do Raw Hamburger Serving

Men usually like this serving with drinks.

1. Buy ground round from best steer beef and spread it on rye-bread slices which have been spread lightly with hot mustard.
2. Make thick servings of the raw meat and top with thin circles of sweet onions. Serve with a smile, even if it doesn't appeal to you!

Be *sure* the meat is freshly-ground and kept in the refrigerator to the minute of serving.

HOW-TO-DO

RUM BALLS (NO COOKING REQUIRED)

(Betty's Unusual Serving for Teleguests)

You will need:

½ pound vanilla wafers	2 tablespoons cocoa
1 cup pecans, finely broken	½ cup white corn sirup
¼ cup rum (dark)	

1. Grind the vanilla wafers fine.
2. Break (*do not* chop) the pecans into very small pieces.
3. Add the cocoa to the ground vanilla wafers.
4. Stir in the corn sirup and the pecans.
5. Now add the rum and stir until well blended.
6. Coat the palms of your hands with confectioners' sugar and roll bits of the mixture into balls about the size of a hazelnut.
7. Let stand an hour or more to form and dry and then roll in confectioners' sugar.

Makes 24 rum balls about the size of a marble.

NOTE: Grand Marnier, Kirsch, or Curaçao may be used instead of rum.

For Television Guests
To Serve from Snack Bar, Buffet, or on Trays

1. Shrimp dipped in garlic chili sauce and broiled in bacon.

2. Cheese squares with orange mint drink.

3. Homemade vegetable soup.

4. Baked whitefish with hot spoon bread.

5. Applesauce squares and hot spiced tea.

6. Bran rolls, piping hot, with fruit salad.

7. Prosciuto ham and honeydew melon with lime wedge.

8. Wrap *prosciuto* ham around long crusty bread sticks and pile them across one end of narrow tray; next arrange perfect ripe figs on tray; then small glasses for a superb red wine. Delightful, and no trouble. It dents the old budget, but brings much applause!

9. Hot orange rolls with pink grapefruit and avocado salad drenched with Cardinal Dressing (page 76) and served with hot chocolate.

10. Devil's food cake with thick caramel icing served with tall glasses of coffee float topped with Saigon cinnamon.

11. Place on snack bar a big tureen filled with hot split-pea soup with chunks of broiled crab. Also toasted sesame-seed rolls sizzling hot. *To drink:* A jug of cider.

12. Hot tamales and enchiladas.

How-to-do Guacamole

A bowl of *guacamole* is the first serving we run out of at our parties.

Buy really ripe avocados. Mash to a paste, using a silver fork. Add 2 tablespoons each of lemon (or lime) juice, grated onion, and mashed ripe tomato, peeled. Stir in ¼ teaspoon salt and 1 teaspoon minced red-hot pepper. Mix thoroughly and pour into small, *deep* glass bowl. Surround with Fritos. Place a plate of toasted crackers near by. For dipping or spreading.

HOW-TO-DO
"DUNKIN'" SERVING FOR TELEGUESTS

You will need:

2 packages cream cheese	1 teaspoon grated onion
½ teaspoon dry mustard	1 teaspoon paprika
2 tablespoons minced chives	1 tablespoon capers (or pickle relish)
2 tablespoons anchovy paste	
1 tablespoon caraway seeds	Ale

1. Mix all ingredients together and add enough ale to make the mixture light and fluffy when beaten with a fork.

2. Pour into a chilled glass bowl and place the bowl in the center of a large plate.

3. Pile Fritos and crusty bread sticks on the plate around the bowl.

4. Let your teleguests dunk the Fritos or bread sticks into this delicious dunkin'!

Makes a full cup of mixture.

6. Beauties for the Preserve Shelf

HOW-TO-DO PEAR HONEY

This is really an easy jam to make and it's economical, besides being perfectly delicious with hot biscuits, toasted muffins, or even to pour over ice cream for a Sudden Sundae.

You will need:

10 pounds pears   ⅔ pound sugar for each
1 lemon   pound of pears
         1 large can crushed pineapple

1. Peel and core the pears and run them through the food chopper (often I do not peel pears).
2. Place pears, sugar, unpeeled lemon sliced paper-thin, and only enough water to prevent burning in a large kettle.
3. Stir over low heat until sugar is dissolved.

4. Increase heat and boil 20 minutes.

5. Add pineapple and boil gently until fruit is very thick and takes on a transparent quality. Time depends on fruit and size of kettle. But pear honey should be a thick, heavy jam, almost as thick as marmalade.

6. Pour into sterilized jars and seal while hot.

How-to-do Wild Grape Jelly

Down on the Adams farm, deep in the woods near the old log cabin, was a thicket of wild grape vines. Of course the heaviest clusters of grapes hung from the tallest trees, but somehow we managed to get them all. Late in the autumn we began watching them ripen and when the last one was picked and turned into a big kettle for winy jelly, I felt richer than Croesus.

If you can "tree" any wild grapes:

1. Wash and pick off all grapes from their stems.

2. Place in large kettle, not more than half full.

3. Heat gently until steam forms, then mash thoroughly.

4. Increase heat and boil for about half an hour.

5. Turn into jelly bag and let drip overnight.

6. Measure the juice into a large kettle having lots of surface and place over high heat.

7. When juice boils, a real tumbling hard boil,

8. Measure the same number of cups of sugar that you have of juice and begin adding sugar very slowly to the juice, stirring constantly.

9. Test by dropping a little from a spoon onto a saucer.

When it drops in two jellylike, definite drops from the side of the spoon it is done. This takes 8 to 10 minutes, depending on size of kettle and on temperature maintained.

HOW-TO-DO
AUNT SUSAN'S STRAWBERRY PRESERVES
(Super-Special)

When I have finished filling a row of little jars full of big plump whole-strawberry preserves, I feel positively rich. It's an old story in our family that I've never been known to carry a tune, but sometimes, while ladling these rich perfect strawberry preserves up from the tray, I have noticed that I was humming right square on key. One quart strawberries and one quart sugar will give you one pint of strawberry preserves, which money can't buy.

You will need:

    2 pints strawberries, washed and stemmed
    2 pints sugar
    1 pint water

1. Wash berries before removing stems. Wash only a few at a time and don't soak them in water. Drain on soft paper towels.

2. *To measure:* Pile the berries in pint measuring cup until not one more berry will stay on. Measure sugar level.

3. Use a large kettle with plenty of surface (I'm partial to my 12-quart preserving kettle), and place 1 heaping pint of strawberries and 1 level pint of sugar and 1 pint of water in it.

4. Set on low heat until every grain of sugar is dissolved. Shake kettle gently and carefully stir sugar from bottom with a long handled rubber scraper. Don't stir with spoon and break berries.

5. Now increase heat and let preserves come to a good boil. Watch closely and when it actually is boiling, count 10 minutes for boiling time. No more.

6. Lift kettle clear off the range and let all bubbling stop.

7. Now right on top of these cooked berries add 1 pint more of strawberries (heaped high) and 1 pint more of sugar (level). No more water.

8. Return to low heat until sugar is dissolved. Be careful not to stir and mash berries, but use scraper to be sure sugar is all dissolved.

9. Turn heat up and bring to boil. Boil exactly 10 minutes. No longer.

10. Remove white scum which forms on top. Do this while mixture is boiling. Rubber scraper is fine for this too.

11. Set aside in kettle until cool, but not cold. Then turn into shallow trays and let stand 24 hours.

12. Pour, cold, into sterilized jars.

13. Cover with paraffin.

14. Store in cool dark cupboard; not on high shelf, as heat goes up, you know.

These preserves are always perfect if you watch several important things:

Be sure to drain berries after washing and pat dry with paper towels.

Heap them high in measuring cup.

Spread out in shallow trays to stand so berries are in one single layer in sirup.

Turn berries in sirup at least once so they will plump up to their original size.

In damp weather, let berries stand a few hours longer.

Be sure to wash kettle before starting a second batch.

How-to-do Apple Butter

Even in a New York apartment I still make a few jars of this delicious apple butter. Twice, now, we have had "neighbors" in our apartment building actually stop at our door—once when the black-out siren went off by mistake, and once when I'd just finished eleven half pints of boiled-cider apple butter. Easy as pie to make.

1. Find apples which are tart and juicy and not too ripe.
2. Peel and core them and cut into small pieces.
3. Place in large kettle and cover with good fresh apple cider.
4. Over high heat, bring to a real boil.
5. Turn heat down and simmer gently until the quality of heavy thick sauce. Let cool and measure.
6. To each full quart of the applesauce add 1 cup sugar.
7. Again bring to full rounding boil.
8. Lower heat and simmer until right thickness.
9. Stir frequently.
10. Turn into sterilized jars and seal while hot.

How-to-do Blue Damson Plum Preserves

It's been years since I did much canning. But even in a New York apartment I still make a few jars of blue damson preserves, Aunt Susan's Special Strawberry Preserves, and corn relish. So I'm including these prized recipes for you.

1. Prick the skins of blue damson plums all around each plum.
2. Place 2¼ pounds of sugar in a large kettle and add 1½ cups water. Stir over moderate heat until every bit of sugar is dissolved.
3. Bring to a good rolling boil and add 3 pounds blue damson plums.
4. Let it come back to boil for a few minutes, then turn heat to low-moderate and cook slowly until the plums are tender and the pits burst from their skins and come to the top to be scooped out. The sirup will drop from the side of the spoon in 2 jellylike drops when the plums are done.
5. Turn into sterilized jars and seal.

Mighty good with chicken or pork.

HOW-TO-DO MY COMPANY CONSERVE

When I plan a company dinner, it usually means I'll argue about what goes into my favorite crystal compote dish. Shall I use spiced blue damson plums, or is the occasion festive enough to sacrifice another jar of my own strawberry preserves? Or maybe my luscious Company Conserve fits better.

Anyhow, it's important to offer spiced preserves or a

jam or jelly which will be remembered. These old recipes of mine will never fail you and they should make your menus famous.

You will need:

2 dozen ripe peaches	1 pound Thompson seed-
1 dozen red plums	less grapes
6 nectarines	4 teaspoons lemon juice
2 oranges	1 cup broken pecans
1 large ripe pineapple	
(page 37)	

1. Wash the fruit and remove seeds, but do not peel any of it except the pineapple. Leave grapes whole.

2. Cut into large even cubes. Avoid getting pieces too small or mixture will be mushy.

3. Place fruit in large preserving kettle having plenty of surface.

4. Cook over very low heat until the juice begins to flow from the fruit. Remove from heat.

5. Now measure the fruit and for each cup of fruit allow ¾ cup sugar.

6. Return fruit to kettle and place over low heat, adding the sugar slowly so that it dissolves readily. Do not stir or fruit will be mushy. Just shake the kettle frequently and keep that heat low until all sugar is dissolved.

7. Now bring it to the boiling point, then reduce the heat to simmering and cook for about 2 hours.

8. Ten minutes before time is up, add 4 teaspoons lemon juice and the broken pecans.

9. Set aside for several hours until cold, then pour into sterilized jars and cover with paraffin.

HOW-TO-DO
MY TWENTY-MINUTE PRESERVES

This is such an easy recipe to follow that my brides always stock their shelves with cherry, dewberry, peach, and apricot preserves. Each is made by this same recipe.

2 pints fruit (measured after   2 pints sugar
   pits are removed. Save all
   juice)

NOTE: No water is used in this recipe.

1. Place fruit in preserving kettle with plenty of surface. Pour sugar over it.
2. Set over low heat until sugar is dissolved, then bring to a boil. Boil gently for 20 minutes.
3. At the end of this time the sirup will sheet from the spoon and fall in two jellylike drops. A few minutes longer may be required, but avoid overcooking or preserves will be tough.
4. Set aside in pan until cold.
5. Then turn into sterilized jars and cover with paraffin.

HOW-TO-DO CORN RELISH

You will need:

6 ears of corn	3 small hot red peppers
½ pound cucumbers	1 small bunch celery
½ pound white onions	1 teaspoon turmeric
1½ pounds tomatoes	1 quart vinegar
2 green peppers	2½ tablespoons salt
2 sweet red peppers	2 cups sugar

5 tablespoons whole light mustard seed

1. Peel peppers and remove seeds and fiber. Peel cucumbers, onions, and tomatoes. Dice in small even cubes. Use a knife to chop all vegetables, NOT a food chopper. Cut *inside* stalks of celery in small pieces.

2. Stir turmeric with a little vinegar and mix till smooth.

3. Add to remaining vinegar with salt, sugar, and mustard seed and stir until dissolved.

4. In a large kettle, combine vegetables and vinegar mixture.

5. Bring to good boil and then cook at moderate heat, not boiling, for 1 hour.

6. Stir gently frequently, but don't mash.

7. When done, pack while boiling hot into 3 hot sterilized jars.

8. Fill jars to the top and seal at once.

HOW-TO-DO STUFFED PICKLED CUCUMBERS

These make superb crisp pickle rings. I always make plenty and include one or two jars in Christmas packages.

You will need:

6 large long cucumbers	½ pound seedless raisins
1 cup salt	4 cups sugar
16 cups water	2 cups vinegar
½ tablespoon alum (drugstore)	½ tablespoon whole cloves
1 large lemon	2 sticks cinnamon

Be sure to buy fresh cucumbers, just gathered, and select straight, long, even ones. Important.

1. Wash cucumbers and cut about 1½-inch piece from each end.

2. Scoop out seed portion, leaving a cavity the full length of the cucumber. An iced-tea spoon is a good tool to use for this.

3. Replace the ends and fasten with toothpicks.

4. Lay cucumbers flat in large bowl or stand them in a gallon jar. Be sure to keep ends in place.

5. Add salt to 8 cups of water and bring to boiling point and pour over cucumbers to cover. Put a lid on jar.

6. Let stand in cool place 12 days. Not in refrigerator. If no basement, try the floor in a ventilated closet.

7. Drain and rinse quickly in cold water.

8. Return to crock or jar and add alum to 8 cups cold water and pour it over the cucumbers.

9. Let stand 24 hours.

10. Drain and cover again with cold water and let stand another 24 hours.

11. Chop lemon, including rind, and mix with raisins. Now stuff this into the cucumbers and fasten the ends back securely with toothpicks.

12. Combine sugar, vinegar, cloves, and cinnamon and bring to boiling point.

13. Pour hot mixture over cucumbers in jar.

14. Place weight over cucumbers to hold them down in the vinegar mixture and let stand overnight.

15. For the next nine mornings pour the sirup off into
    a saucepan and heat it to boiling and quickly pour
    it back over pickles. Cover jar.

They keep indefinitely in their rich spicy sirup and
are simply luscious, besides being beautiful. Slice into
thick circles to serve. Sounds like trouble, but requires
only a few minutes each day and they are worth it.

7. Menus
the Home Freeze Way

If I could do exactly what I'd love to do—do you know what would happen? I'd enclose a home freezer with each one of these books. Then cooking would be turned into a real production and homemaking would very quickly become a recognized business. Well, that will come, just don't be too impatient!

When you have a home freezer, complete menus are prepared and tucked away for the many days you do NO cooking.

You'll find a good buy on lamb some Tuesday morning. So buy two legs of lamb. Roast one and freeze it for some future dinner. Have the second one boned and cut into big bite-sized chunks. Here you have two *shish kebab* dinners, one for today, one for another menu.

Marinate these pieces in oil, wine and vinegar mixed,

or just wine if you prefer, with oregano, salt, and pepper. Freeze half of the purchase and you are all set for *shish kebab*.

Or, prepare that second leg o' lamb as a delicious fricassee. Marinate it the same way; drain, brown, and simmer till tender. Finish with carrots, onions, and tomatoes to serve on top of brown rice. Make lots of spicy gravy.

Of course, if there is no home freezer yet, you can try these same suggestions in the freezing unit in your refrigerator. A limited amount may be handled.

Dinner from the Home Freezer

Roast Guinea
Add Baked Potatoes
Broccoli and Hollandaise
Add Fennel   Radishes   Gherkins
Apple Pie and Ice Cream
Hot Tea

*   *   *

Fowl and meats can be roasted ready to serve and stowed away for a special dinner. I slip a menu in with them and am ready pronto, with no knitting of brows.

Cakes and pies can be frozen and we think they are really better for their "ripening" process.

Always double the recipe for egg cutlets (page 237) and add chicken sometimes, for they are also better for a watchful waiting spell.

Buy grapefruit when it's plentiful and at its best and stow away cartons and cartons of sections for salads and for good plain eating by itself.

Long ago I learned about the frozen-onion department and how I do bless this friend for showing me how to buy those sweet Spanish onions in quantities and chop, mince, onion-ring, and grate them into various-sized packages for future use. Try it.

Home Freeze Menus Ready to Heat and Serve

Roast Long Island Duck with Orange
Sweet Potatoes
Corn on Cob
All Bran Rolls
Add Green Salad and Plain French Dressing
Frozen Angel Food Cake (page 198) with Orange Glaze
Coffee

This home freeze menu was the very first show I ever did on television. Everyone approved.

* * *

(frozen) Braised Beef Shoulder (gravy frozen)
Frozen Limas
(frozen) Fruit Salad   *Add* Celery and Olives
(frozen) Apple Dumplings with Orange Pastry
(frozen) Coffee

* * *

Egg Cutlets (page 237) with Chicken Added
Frozen Peas and Tiny White Onions Cooked in Cream
Add Avocado, Grapefruit (frozen sections) Salad, and
Cardinal Dressing (page 76)
Frozen Pound Cake
Frozen Custard Ice Cream
Coffee

8. Finds That Have Been Tested by Generations of Homemakers

Finds are usually so simple nobody ever bothers to tell the new homemaker about them. There are many scattered through the pages of this book. And here now is a special collection that seemed to fit just anywhere but nowhere. When you've used one of these finds three times it's yours, so help yourself daily.

Lay an orange peel on the burner of your range and let it burn slowly. The aroma is delightful and helps to dispel fish, cabbage, and other strong smells.

Long ago I bought a stack of roomy, lightweight trays. I keep these in a rack in the kitchen and it is routine for each member of the family to come to the kitchen and help themselves to breakfast served on their special tray. Each one carries his tray to a favorite spot and eats in peace. Strangely enough, there is nothing left on these trays and formerly breakfast was merely picked at. Try it a few times and see how your youngsters enjoy reading or doing a last-minute bit of studying as they eat. Dad will not feel guilty if he reads his paper in peace and you will have a whole set of reasons for enjoying this routine.

An interesting centerpiece: Heap velvety bright-red cockscomb on one side of a copper plate or tray. Across the remaining half of the plate arrange bunches of big black grapes, letting them fall from the edge of plate.

Remember that wine cooked in food accents the salt, so I'm careful to add salt last and taste to be sure.

For an emergency cheese sauce, just dump a package of process cheese into the top of a double boiler with 1/3 cup cold milk. Stir over hot, not boiling, water until cheese is melted.

When soft-cooking or hard-cooking eggs, always steal a minute to run hot water over them if you take them from the refrigerator, then place one by one in bowl of a tablespoon and lower into hot water. No cracking now.

When hard-cooking eggs, never stack them in saucepan. When poaching eggs always be sure that water in skillet will completely cover eggs.

Try frying eggs with a tight lid on skillet—Surprise.

Remove hard-cooked eggs from heat when done and hold under cold-water faucet. Then crack egg shell all around till completely loosened and peel under cold-water faucet.

To open hot soft-cooked eggs easily, fold a piece of soft paper on the bias and wrap folded edge to fit around lower portion of egg. With sharp whack of table knife, cut across large end and using pointed iced-tea spoon dip egg out of shell into heated cup. Iced-tea spoon fits inside of shell without breaking it.

Muffins, pancakes, and waffles require the least mixing possible. Overmixing or too much stirring and beating ruins the results. No tunnels or leathery cracked tops in muffins if you watch those strokes. The fewer strokes you make, the lighter the pancakes and waffles.

Fried apples are so good for breakfast surprises and easy to do. Just core apple, but don't peel. Cut into slices about 1/4 inch thick. Use skillet with large surface. Heat butter to bubble; do not brown. Add apples, not stacked, and fry gently. Brown on both sides, turning with a broad pancake turner to avoid breaking them. Remove to hot plate and dust lightly with granulated sugar and a shake of nutmeg.

Did you ever slice salt pork into thin slices, dip it in buttermilk, drain it, then roll it in white corn meal and fry it in hot bacon drippings quickly? Mighty good. The old South makes cream gravy of the leavings after frying salt pork. It's served with fluffy hot biscuits.

Add a dash of curry powder to scrambled eggs. It gives them such a zip!

Mix 2 teaspoons of cinnamon with ½ cup honey and pour into small jars to use on hot buttered toast or waffles.

Just buy a dime's worth of good-quality caramels, dark and light for flavor. Drop them into the top of a double boiler with ½ cup hot water. Stir a few times, letting caramels dissolve slowly. This makes a smooth delicious sauce which is so good poured over ice-cream desserts, puddings, cake, or whatever occurs to you.

Before measuring molasses, dip the measuring spoon or cup into hot water so that the molasses flows out easily.

When making Parker House rolls, be sure to snip them with the scissors right in the fold, making a half-inch opening or "hinge." Press the edges closely together and they will not pop open as they bake.

Use paper cups to bake cup cakes and they don't even need greasing.

Fruit cake should never be stored in same container with bread or with other cake. It deserves a special container with a tight lid. Add an orange or sliced apple for moisture, but don't forget to change the apple slices every few days.

Use a heated knife to slice fresh bread and the loaf doesn't lose its shape.

There is a vast difference in pimiento and pimento. PIMIENTO is the delicately flavored bright-red sweet pepper. PIMENTO is a spice.

Don't say SAV-OR-Y. It's SĀ-VOR-Y, with a long A.

Actually it's incorrect to say "boiled custard," because it must NEVER boil. That's what makes it curdle.

It is incorrect to say soft- or hard-boiled eggs, because they must NEVER boil. Maybe if we would *say* soft- or hard-cooked that's what would happen.

Good cinnamon toast is a luxury to be found at home only. I've ordered it in the most famous and expensive restaurants and invariably it was half brother to a brown blotter, slightly warmed. All you have to do is toast thin slices of bread on one side under the broiler. Remove bread and spread untoasted side with cinnamon-toast mix. Return to broiler rack and toast the mixture into the surface until it forms a glazed, bubbly crust. DON'T STACK TOAST OF ANY KIND.
Cinnamon Toast Mix: Cream together 6 tablespoons of softened butter and 1 cup confectioners' sugar which has been sifted with 2 tablespoons cinnamon. *To vary:*

Add broken pecans, or slivers of candied ginger, or occasionally use Saigon cinnamon for a thrill.

The olden cookbooks' direction for flavoring was "Add the zest of one lemon, or one orange." This is good to remember, because only the zest, or the pungent oily quality in the yellow rind, is flavorful. Do NOT grate down into the white membrane or a bitterness is added.

How To Grate Lemon or Orange Rind

1. See page 18 for graters. Use fine grater.
2. Hold grater over a piece of waxed paper.
3. Lightly grate the lemon or orange rind over grater, being very careful to cut no deeper than the oily yellow portion. Use light quick strokes and the grating will go through onto paper instead of sticking to grater.
4. Using a fork, remove every bit of rind from grater. Scrape all rind and oil from paper into sauce or icing. As you sniff the fragrance of this zest, you'll see why it adds so much to so many servings.

You will need to remember that 2 tablespoons (1 envelope) of gelatin will thicken 4 cups of liquid. Always follow directions on the package for using gelatin and also for Jello mixtures.

When a recipe says *heat* butter to fry or sauté eggs or any other food it will help if you remember that the butter must *never* brown. So keep that heat moderately low. A few recipes call for browned butter, but they are specials.

Keep a custard cup filled with orange-toast mix in your refrigerator. All you have to do is cream ½ stick of softened butter with 1 cup confectioners' sugar, add the grated rind of an orange (or more), and then stir in orange juice until mixture is about the consistency of honey. Spread this on hot toast and run slices under the broiler a minute. Serve hot for breakfast, tea, snacks, or midnight prowls.

To keep your mixing bowl steady when whipping or mixing ingredients, place the bowl on a folded damp cloth.

If your refrigerator is small, conserve space by removing the rind from cantaloupe, cutting it into slim sections, and storing in a covered jar just ready to serve.

Do you have scales in your kitchen? Let me urge you to add scales to your equipment. You can check meat, fowl, and fish to know what you've bought and to know how to estimate cooking time. My kitchen scales are now fifteen years old and have paid for themselves many, many times.

That Good Tight Lid

This is my theme song through countless recipes. I've learned it is basic in mastering many servings. Strangely, it isn't emphasized strongly enough to impress all homemakers sufficiently.

That is why I repeat it so often and insist on using a good tight-seal lid each time it is important.

For example:

Long ago I was trying to help one of my brides learn to prepare meat perfectly. She seemed unable to braise a juicy, tender beef-rump roast and insisted that I just got better meat than she was able to buy.

Finally I watched her prepare the meat. She had my recipe and thought she was following instructions. When she came to the place where it said "Cover with tight lid" she turned a skillet upside down over the roaster, because the lid was lost. Of course the steam was not held inside the roaster, but escaped rapidly. The liquid was reduced and the meat dried out as it cooked.

Now I urge you to buy a small roaster, or Dutch oven, or both, which has a good tight-seal lid. Also buy two or three saucepans with good tight-seal lids. Use them when directed.

"That good tight lid" is a constant refrain in my How-TO-DO helps. A good tight-seal lid is a must in braising meats because every bit of steam is held in the pan, less liquid is used, the meat does not dry out, and the heavy connective tissue is gently dissolved by long, slow, moist cookery.

Rice is a different serving when closely covered with that tight-seal lid and all the steam softens the hard rice grains, instead of escaping into the room.

Dried fruits plump up and are as full of juice as they were when picked from the tree if gently simmered, with a good tight lid on the saucepan.

If you don't have a heavy skillet with a seal lid, a heavy saucepan with a seal lid, and some kind of Dutch oven, just remind yourself that these are basic equipment and you must buy them. Why not today?

Use Scissors

To mince parsley, chives, green peppers, pimiento, marshmallows, dates.

How To Stir

Recently I asked one of the girls in the studio to stir some brown sugar and cream and butter for me. This mixture was starting to cook over low heat. She turned the heat up and gingerly pushed the sugar around with the tip end of her spoon.

When I quickly showed her how to stir by placing the bottom of the spoon against the bottom of the pan and moving the mixture round and round over low heat till every grain of sugar was dissolved she was pleased. But she asked why nobody had ever told her that before.

Of course they have, because when recipes say "Stir carefully over low heat" they mean just that.

These basic How-to-do's are designed to give you a pattern which is step by step. This pattern is perfect. It works and you may use it for all your cookery. You'll suddenly pay better attention to all recipe directions when you know basic rules for basic cooking.

Turn the Heat Low and Simmer

These are also theme songs you'll find stressed repeatedly in my basic-cookery directions.

When I was a very small youngster, I can recall Mama saying to me "Go in the kitchen and turn that heat down under the mush [or the dried apricots, or the meat]" and once I asked her how she knew it always needed to be turned down instead of up.

She just said I could always remember that anything which cooked very long needed to simmer gently until done. This is still the best rule I can give you.

"Put on an apron, kids" was another reminder she insisted on when we started toward the kitchen. That's also a good one for you to adopt.

How to Use a Pastry Cloth

I wish I could give pastry cloths out with every marriage license issued. If this were possible, brides would begin making good pastry instead of having so many problems with it.

May I urge you to get a pastry cloth before you attempt another pie? I've made hundreds of pies and never have a failure. I use a pastry cloth every single time.

A pastry cloth is heavy canvas. It may be placed flat on the table and no board is required. Rub flour into the cloth, rubbing hard until all the mesh is filled with flour. It feels like velvet and acts like a blotter for the soft dough. Rub flour into your rolling-pin cover the same way.

When the pastry is mixed into a ball as directed in my recipe, turn it onto this pastry cloth and roll as directed. The sheet of pastry does not take up any flour at all. It does not stick and you are able to handle it quickly and lightly.

The pastry cloth serves as a blotter for biscuit dough, doughnut dough, cooky dough, or dough for hot rolls. None of them should have any flour at all added as they are rolled or handled.

Using a spatula, scrape all the flour off the cloth when finished. Shake the cloth and roll it around the rolling pin and wrap in waxed paper to put away for next time. Cloth needs washing very seldom.

Don'ts to Dot!

I have always kept a bulletin board in my kitchen. On this the whole family posted notes, telling their whereabouts, giving instructions for the cleaner, saying why they didn't do their chores, and to please call them at 6:45 on the day of the home-coming game!

Also I wrote notes to various maids and they left me some, which should fill a book of smiles and hearty laughs. Dot was one who topped them all. I finally concluded that she thought in reverse, but oh how she made the dishes and silver and copper shine! Also, she never failed to arrive on the day expected. So I wrote and re-wrote "Don'ts to Dot."

It seems like a good idea to include them here, because I firmly believe you are not likely to ask a question or make a mistake which Dot overlooked.

DOT . . . *Don't leave spice boxes open.*

DOT . . . *Please don't leave spice boxes or jars on that shelf over the range.*

DOT . . . *Don't put bacon in the freezer unit of the refrigerator.*

DOT . . . *Don't . . . PLEASE . . . don't leave ANY food in paper sacks in refrigerator.*

DOT . . . *Please don't throw my good sharp knives into this drawer. Remember the knife rack.*

DOT . . . *Don't fail to check the clothes twice before putting them into the washer. You left a red scarf in a blouse pocket. That's what turned it pink.*

DOT . . . *Don't use such a heavy coating of wax on the furniture. Only a very light film is necessary.*

DOT . . . *Don't leave those oily rags in the closet under the sink. They are perfect fire starters. Throw them out or wash them.*

DOT . . . *Don't believe in luck in cooking . . . you have to think.*

DOT . . . *Don't remove the aluminum foil from those lemons in the refrigerator. The paper keeps lemons moist and fresh.*

DOT . . . *Please don't forget to keep garbage bags in our new $5.00 can . . . or it will soon be worth only about 5¢.*

DOT . . . *Heat butter soft biscuit-color, but it must never scorch. Don't heat butter too hot.*

DOT . . . *Don't let tables go so long without waxing. Stains and water rings mar the surface of the wood. Keep wax on for protection.*

DOT . . . *Please don't turn the heat up to hurry a stew, or braising, or soup, or rice . . . or any simmering food. . . . TIME, not high heat, tenderizes meat and softens dried food.*

DOT . . . *Don't take the lemon out of my brown-sugar jar. I leave it there to keep the brown sugar soft. Keep lid on tightly, too.*

DOT . . . *Don't stack cheese and bacon and other packaged foods on refrigerator shelves. The cold air must circulate around food or it isn't kept cold.*

*   *   *

Allow ¼ to ½ square of chocolate to each cup of milk in chocolate drinks. Allow 3 teaspoons of cocoa to each cup of milk for drinks.

Did you know that it takes five quarts of milk to make a pound of cheese? No wonder we are urged to use cheese and use it again in menus.

Always serve cheese at room temperature.

The gourmet prefers fruit at room temperature. All the fine flavor is pointed up when fruit is eaten as it comes from the tree.

And watermelon . . . Well of course there really is just one way to eat watermelon and that's out in the back yard. Bring the big dark-green melon right from the spring house and cut it (hear it rip?) into big long wedges. Hold in your two hands and go straight across. Let the seeds fall where they may.

One cup uncooked rice equals 3 cups cooked and serves 4.

Macaroni, spaghetti, and noodles double in bulk after cooking. 8-ounce package serves 4.

Now here is a real find and a bright spot in 1951: A grand range with an oven I can stand and look into. Yes. I mean that NOW I do not have to stand on my head to see what is happening inside the oven or the broiler. Progress.

When you are preparing iced coffee for a large group it's hard on the ice-cube situation. Have you tried frozen coffee concentrate? You'll be surprised, for it makes delicious iced coffee. I use three times the amount called for and sometimes I add milk instead of water. Delicious. (This from a black-coffee fan and a crank about her coffee.)

Someday I'm going to have (1) all the flowers I want, (2) a horse to ride every day, (3) all the black walnuts I need, (4) all the Jonathan apples I can eat and cook, (5) a nonleak fountain pen with a Spencerian point. What are your five foolish fancies?

Do treat yourself and your family to those luscious big golden persimmons which are on our markets for a few brief weeks in the winter. The flavor and quality and color are simply exquisite. Sometimes I get them just dead ripe and they're so soft I have to spoon them out of the skins. What to do? Stir this flavorful pulp through *good* vanilla ice cream and serve topped with two or three sections of the persimmon, or even with a spoonful of the pulp. Nice. Also add the pulp or the whole sections to fruit salad for a true lilt.

How to Fold?

Fold stiffly beaten egg whites through cake batter, for example. Using large slotted spoon, cut stiffly beaten whites down through batter, gently cutting them across, up, over, down, across, up, and over. Make each motion count as you are combining "air bubbles" with the batter.

How to Beat?

Beat through the batter, beating air into it and mixing ingredients at the same time.

How to Stir?

To stir sugar and water together over low heat, keep the bottom of the spoon on bottom of the pan and *stir* with circular motion. Include sides of pan and keep mixture moving.

How-to-do Onion Juice?

Cut thick slice from large sweet onion. Use orange or lemon reamer and squeeze juice from onion as from an orange.

How to Keep Cantaloupe in Small Refrigerator

Cut cantaloupe into sections. Remove seed and pare all rind from each section, leaving only edible melon. Fit into jar and cover with tight lid. Or use a baking dish with tight cover. Store in refrigerator. No odor at all.

9. Additional Recipes

HOW-TO-DO SUSAN'S ORANGE MINT DRINK

Everybody in Oklahoma and Texas drinks Aunt Susan's Orange Mint!

All through the scorching hot days of their long summers these Southwestern homemakers make up quarts of "that orange mint drink" and they keep it in the refrigerator from May till November. This has been going on in the Great Southwest since the year 1929 and no drink has ever displaced it.

2½ cups water	Grated rind and juice of 2
2 cups sugar	oranges
2 handfuls of mint	Juice of 6 lemons

1. Boil sugar and water together for 5 minutes to make thin sirup.
2. Pour boiling sirup over crushed mint leaves and stems in deep mixing bowl.
3. Cover mixture with tight lid and let it stand to steep for at least 30 minutes. Longer time is better.

4. Add juice and grated rind to mint sirup.

5. Strain into tall jar and place in refrigerator.

6. *To serve:* Fill tall glasses with powdered ice. Pour 1/3 cup (5 tablespoons plus 1 teaspoon) of sirup over powdered ice and fill glasses with ice water or with soda or ginger ale. Add straws.

Refreshing and delicious.

IMPORTANT NOTE: Directions say to fill tall glasses with *powdered* ice. That does NOT mean cubes, chunks, or cracked ice. It's not the same drink over anything but powdered ice, which is ice crushed as fine as possible—almost like snow. I have crushers, blenders, and other ice gadgets, but nothing beats a tough canvas bag, an ice mallet or hammer, and the back-porch steps.

HOW-TO-DO BERT'S EGGNOG

NOTE TO SUSAN: *As you already know, I've made this each Christmas Eve more than a quarter of a century and have never had a failure yet.*

You will need:

6 eggs	1 jigger Bacardi rum
1 cup sugar	1 pint whipping cream
1 pint good bourbon	1 pint whole milk

1. Using rotary beater, beat egg yolks until very thick and pale lemon-colored.

2. Add sugar gradually, beating well until all sugar is dissolved. Should be almost jellylike.

3. Add whisky and rum to egg-yolk mixture, pouring it in a very fine stream and beating constantly. This cooks the eggs, so do pour it slowly.

4. In a large bowl, whip the egg whites until stiff and carefully fold into them 1 pint whipped cream. Fold. Do not stir.

5. Now *slowly* pour the egg-yolk mixture into the foamy egg white and cream mixture, folding carefully until perfectly mixed.

6. Thin with milk to consistency you like.

7. Set into refrigerator to ripen at least an hour, or more.

8. Serve in red eggnog mugs. Sprinkle with nutmeg.

HOW-TO-DO AUNT BILL'S BROWN CANDY

To begin with, let me tell you that this makes more than three pounds of candy, so you see it is not as expensive as it might seem.

You will find it much easier to manage if two of you are able to make it together, but this is not necessary. I've made loads of it alone.

You will need:

3 pints white sugar
1 pint whole milk (or cream)
¼ teaspoon soda
¼ pound butter
1 teaspoon vanilla
1 pound pecans

1. Pour one pint of sugar into a heavy aluminum or iron skillet and place over low heat.

2. Begin stirring with a wooden spoon and keep sugar moving so it will not scorch at all. It will take 15 minutes to melt all the sugar completely and at no time let it smoke or cook so fast that it turns dark. It should be about the color of light brown sugar sirup.

3. As soon as you have the sugar heating, pour the remaining two pints of sugar together with the pint of milk or cream into a deep, heavy kettle and set it over low heat to cook slowly while you are melting the sugar in the skillet.

4. As soon as all the sugar is melted, begin pouring it into the kettle of boiling milk and sugar, keeping it on very low heat and stirring constantly. The real secret of mixing these ingredients is to pour a very fine stream from the skillet. Aunt Bill always said to pour a stream no larger than a knitting needle and to stir across the bottom of the kettle all the time.

5. Continue cooking and stirring until mixture forms a firm ball when dropped into cold water, 245 degrees.

6. After this test is made, turn out the fire and immediately add the soda, stirring hard as it foams up.

7. As soon as the soda is mixed, add the butter, allowing it to melt as you stir.

8. Now set off the heat (not outdoors, or in a cold place) for about 20 minutes, until lukewarm. Then add vanilla.

9. Using a wooden spoon, beat until the mixture is thick and heavy, having a dull appearance instead of a glossy sheen.

10. Add broken pecan meats and mix.

11. Turn into tin boxes or square pans, where it may be cut into squares when cooled.

This keeps moist and delicious indefinitely. Decorate

with halves of pecans and you have a most attractive candy.

HOW-TO-DO OUR CHRISTMAS ROCKS

Nettie, my faithful little secretary for so many years, used to say she would be rich if she had a dime for every time she had written this recipe. Homemakers never felt they were ready for the holidays without these flavorful small fruit cakes.

You will need:

¾ cups sugar
¼ cup butter
2 eggs
1½ cups flour
2 teaspoons cocoa
½ teaspoon each cinnamon, mace, nutmeg
½ teaspoon each ginger, allspice

½ teaspoon soda
1 tablespoon strong coffee
1 teaspoon vanilla
¼ cup currants
¼ cup raisins
¼ pound each candied cherries, candied pineapple, citron, orange peel, and dates
½ pound pecans

1. Cream butter and sugar together until light and puffy. This is important.
2. Beat eggs until very foamy, using rotary beater.
3. Sift all dry ingredients together (8 of them).
4. Next add about ½ cup of the flour to the butter and sugar mixture and beat well.
5. Then add the beaten eggs, the vanilla, and the coffee, beating until well mixed.
6. Take out ½ cup of the flour and dredge the nuts and the fruits, which have been cut into slivers (leave currants and raisins whole and break pecan halves in two).

7. Now add remaining flour, being sure to use all that was left from dredging fruits and nuts.

8. Mix and beat thoroughly.

9. Drop by teaspoons onto lightly greased cooky sheet. Leave space between them, as they spread some.

10. Bake at 325 degrees for 12 to 15 minutes. *Don't* brown.

11. Pack in stone or glass jar with tight lid. Sprinkle with brandy and keep for holiday fare. Or place a whole apple or an orange in jar with them. Put fresh fruit in every week.

Next time you'll double the recipe!

How-to-do Amy's Lemon Butter

My husband says he can remember his mother making this "spread" when he was a small boy and she made it for us recently at seventy-seven years young. Her recipe is changeless.

1. In top of double boiler, beat 3 eggs slightly.

2. Whip 5 tablespoons of butter with 1½ cups sugar, making mixture as smooth and light as for a cake.

3. Stir this into the eggs and beat hard.

4. Now beat in 1 tablespoon grated lemon rind and ½ cup lemon juice.

5. Cook over hot, not boiling, water until it begins to thicken and is clear.

6. Remove to small jar. Cover. It gets quite thick when cold. Be careful to keep water below boiling or it will curdle.

Makes about 1½ cups.

HOW-TO-DO EDITH'S CHRISTMAS CANDY

This is such an easy candy to make. It never fails, and how really wonderful it is for holiday offerings!

You will need:

PART ONE

3 cups sugar
1 cup white corn sirup
1 cup cream

1. Mix these 3 ingredients and stir well over low heat until sugar is dissolved.

2. Then boil until soft ball is formed when a little is dropped into cold water (242 degrees).

3. Let it set until lukewarm, then beat until thick and heavy.

4. Now pour it onto porcelain-topped table, bread board, or even a heavy, damp tea towel. Work it with your hands till it is as smooth and firm as cooky dough.

5. Form into 2 long rolls and let set on sheets of waxed paper until perfectly firm.

PART TWO

6. Mix 3 cups of light brown sugar with 1 cup milk and 1/3 cup butter.

7. Stir over low heat until every grain of sugar is dissolved.

8. Increase heat and cook until soft ball is formed in cold water.

9. Let this cool to lukewarm. Then beat until it is thick enough to spread. (It will not be nearly as thick as the liquid in Part One.)

10. Using a spatula, spread this thick coating over the firm rolls. Cover them generously and roll them over to take up all of the thick, shiny glaze.

11. Next, roll these long glazed rolls in a mound of broken pecans until they are completely covered.

12. Turn onto waxed paper and set in a cold dry place (not refrigerator) for several hours, or overnight, before cutting. Serve in thick round slices.

Luscious.

HOW-TO-DO OPAL'S STRAWBERRY DESSERT

You will need:

1 large box strawberries, very ripe	½ cup sugar
	8 marshmallows
1 cup whipping cream	

1. Wash berries and mash.

2. Add sugar and marshmallows and let stand 1 hour.

3. Whip cream (not stiff).

4. Fold it into strawberry mixture.

5. Turn into trays to freeze.

6. Stir two or three times. This is a rough-textured cream, but not icy.

7. Slice very ripe fresh pineapple into thick slices. Peel and remove core section.

8. Dust lightly with sugar and let stand outside the refrigerator until sugar is melted.

9. Chill.

10. Place pineapple slice on chilled dessert plate.

11. Pile strawberry cream in center and garnish with a whole strawberry, stem intact.

Serves 4.

How-to-do Eloise's Summer Dessert

1. Wash and stem Thompson seedless grapes to measure 2 pints.

2. Stir them into 1 cup of sour cream.

3. Turn into glass bowl and dust generously on top with brown sugar. Then dust freshly grated nutmeg over all. Unusual and perfectly delicious.

Serves 4.

How-to-do Muriel's English Guard Sauce

1. Using a fork, whip a glass of red-currant jelly until broken into bits.

2. Add 1 dessert spoon of English Worcestershire sauce.

3. Stir in 1 cup drained black cherries cut in halves. Mix well.

4. Place in refrigerator to chill overnight.

The jelly will set again and is wonderful over baked ham.

How-to-do
Phyllis' Quick Centerpiece for Company Dinner

1. Buy one bunch of small sweetheart roses and cut them with the stems only about 1 inch long.

2. Put 2 trays of ice cubes in an icebag, or in a heavy towel.

3. Pound into small pieces with ice mallet and place in the center of a pretty low silver or glass container.

4. Press the ice with your hands into a very firm cone shape.

5. Stick the rose stems into the cracks of ice all over the cone and then put the whole arrangement into the refrigerator until you're ready to light the candles and call the guests.

The candlelight against the crushed ice and small drops of water on the pale pink and white blossoms makes a pretty picture.

How-to-do Phyllis' Fruit Ice with Sparkling Wine

This is easy to do, can be prepared in advance, and is really inexpensive, although it sounds extravagant. Low on calories, if that makes you enjoy it more.

1. Either make a quart of your own favorite lemon, lime, or pineapple sherbet or buy a container of it at the drugstore.

2. Empty it into a bowl and add 1½ cups of fresh, frozen, or canned fruits cut in small pieces and drained of all juice. Peaches, pears, apricots, raspberries, Queen Anne cherries, or any combination you like.

3. Mix the fruit through the sherbet and turn it into the refrigerator trays to freeze.

4. Chill a bottle of good white table wine.

5. When you are ready to serve the dessert, pour the cold wine into a seltzer bottle.

6. Fill the sherbet dishes about two thirds full of frozen fruit sherbet.

7. Squirt about 1/3 cupful of white wine from the seltzer bottle over the sherbet.

Appropriate, impressive, and easy for a reception for two hundred guests or a dinner for two. I have served this from a lovely antique silver compote, from my prized Steuben bowl, and from a fragrant golden hollowed-out pineapple.

I've also filled the dessert dishes from the refrigerator tray in the kitchen!

This is my budget version of a very expensive dessert served with vintage champagne which I used to eat once in a while in a small restaurant close to the Opéra in Paris.

GRAYACRES ROSE JAR

Early morning is rose-harvest time, before the hot sun extracts too much of the fragrance, but not until the dew has disappeared. The full bloom as well as the bud is good, with the stamen ripe enough to be plucked from the stem with the petals. Just hold the whole thing and pull the blossom off as you do when you're picking cotton.

Spread thinly in an open suit box and sprinkle liberally with salt (do not use iodine-treated salt as it gives a peculiar odor after being closed up tightly). Set in a sunny dry place and toss around every other day until quite dry.

When perfectly dry, place a layer of leaves in a jar, sprinkle well with all kinds of ground spices, then repeat until the jar is filled. Over this, pour a tablespoon of your favorite toilet water or perfume and keep closed, except on rare occasions.

It is best to place the petals in a suit box or on white paper, as they will absorb some of the odor of ink from newspapers.

Dark-colored roses are prettier and retain their richness better than the light-colored blossoms.

Blue larkspur blossoms retain their color and add much to the combination. A few honeysuckle petals are delightful as an addition, also.

Index